# Forty-four Walks

## on the

# Isle of Arran

Clan Walk Guides

# Forty-four Walks on the Isle of Arran

### Mary Welsh

*Maps and illustrations by Michael Whittaker*

*Front cover illustration by David Macaulay*

First published Westmorland Gazette, 1989
Revised Edition Published by Clan Books, 1999


ISBN 1 873597 06 1
© Mary Welsh




Clan Book Sales Ltd
Clandon House
The Cross, Doune
Perthshire
FK16 6BE


Printed by
Cordfall Ltd, Glasgow

# Preface

The Isle of Arran, nearly 170 square miles in size, lies in the broad estuary of the Firth of Clyde. In the north of the island tower lofty mountains, and on their steep rock-strewn slopes you will find heather, mosses, lichens, clubmosses and a variety of ferns. This is the territory of the golden eagle, merlin, buzzard, grouse, curlew, raven, wheatear and meadow pipit. Sheep abound and herds of deer roam freely. They are, however, restrained from the lusher, cultivated south by a high deer fence.

A sparkling blue sea teeming with fish surrounds the island. Grey and common seals frequent its shores and an occasional basking shark dallies, seeking plankton. The raised beaches, the hay meadows, the rough pasture and the deciduous woods support a myriad of wild flowers and host an enormous variety of birds. Dragonflies, grasshoppers, bees, wood wasps and small rodents all thrive on the island, which is protected from the worst effects of snow and frost by the caress of the Gulf Stream.

A narrow road encircles the island, hugging the glorious coastline for nearly all its length; two roads, The Ross and The String, connect the west coast with the east. The peace and tranquillity, the flourishing flora and the multitudinous bird life have drawn me back to the island time and again.

This book of walks has been written in response to requests from many friends for details of the birds and plants seen on the lovely walks. In it I have written a little of Arran's past and much of its wonderful present. I have had enormous encouragement from so many people and would like to thank those who have walked with me, my family, my friends and my faithful border collie. I would also like to thank Derrick Warner, Ranger/Naturalist of Brodick Castle; John A. Stuart of the Scottish Tourist Board who sponsored part of this venture; Dr. Hugh McKerrell and staff of Loch Ranza Field Centre who have helped me discover much of Arran's wealth; Derek Butterworth of

3

Coniston who first enthralled me with descriptions of Arran's magic; and finally, but in no way least, Michael Whittaker, who has illustrated the book with such care and sympathy, enhancing all that I have tried to reveal.

I have written this guide book for all who like to walk. There are short walks and long ones. I have tried to describe the terrain accurately, and hope the book will be read before the walker ventures forth. Some walks require tramping over rough ground and some necessitate using hands as well as feet for scrambling. At some times of the year dense, high bracken makes some paths virtually impassable. But I, on the wrong side of fifty, have completed all the walks included.

Take strong waterproofs and, for longer walks, a spare woolly and more than sufficient food and drink. I would recommend walking in boots as the ground can be very wet at times. But rough or smooth, hot or cold, wet or dry, walking on this lovely island is a great joy.

*Bell heather*

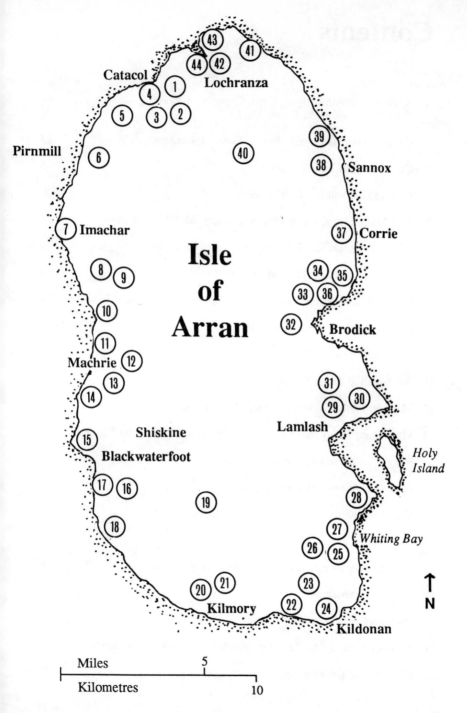

# Contents

# Contents (continued)

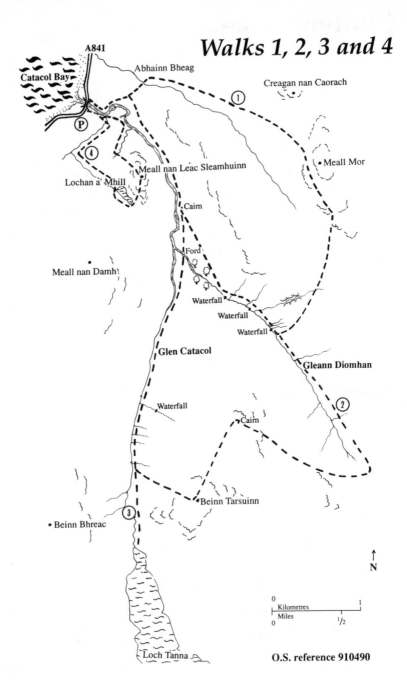

# Walks 1, 2, 3 and 4

A841

Catacol Bay

Abhainn Bheag

Creagan nan Caorach

①

P

Meall Mor

④

Meall nan Leac Sleamhuinn

Lochan a' Mhill

Cairn

Ford

Meall nan Damh

Waterfall

Waterfall

Waterfall

Glen Catacol

Gleann Diomhan

Waterfall

②

Cairn

Beinn Tarsuinn

③

• Beinn Bhreac

N

0          Kilometres          1
0          Miles          ½

Loch Tanna

O.S. reference 910490

# 1. Catacol, Abhainn Bheag Burn, Creag na h-Iolaire, Glen Diomhan, Glen Catacol

Park on the grassy verge south of the Catacol Burn. Walk up the north side of the pebbly river and follow a sheep trod that keeps thirty yards from the farm wall on the left. A young willow warbler with yellow tinted breast sits on a wire above the wall and then aggressively chases away a meadow pipit. Beyond the wall the farmer gathers the last of his hay. Follow a wide track beside

*The track winds behind a ruined cottage*

the wall as it winds behind a ruined cottage and then drops to the edge of a stream. Cross over the hurrying water of Abhainn Bheag Burn. Butterflies and dragon-flies flit over the water where rowans line the banks, and heather, bog myrtle, spearwort, tormentil and meadow vetchling flower.

*Rowan*

Begin to climb, keeping the burn to the right. At first the sheep trods lead through the bracken. Then they come close to a deep gorge. A lovely waterfall leaps down the precipitous slopes in long white tresses past oaks, ashes, service trees and rowans. Then it tumbles once more, lace-like, between the dark walls of the steep-sided ravine into a deep pool. High on a rocky outcrop a congregation of ravens utter deep barks.

Keep well away from the edge of the ravine while climbing the steep hillside, using sheep tracks where possible. Pause often and look back at the lovely view of Catacol below. A small boat sails slowly, leaving feathery ripples in its wake. The calls of oyster-catchers, gulls and curlews on the shore can still be heard. Heather and bleached grass soon replace bracken but male fern continues to grow. The chirping of grasshoppers resounds in the summer's air and the insects jump among the heather to the bewilderment of the writer's dog. Pause again and enjoy the ever-extending views of the mountains of Jura, Mull and the mainland.

Cross the burn at a suitable place when the slopes of Meall Mor come into view and strike up the grassy hillside that leads towards the highest point, marked by a cairn, above the precipitous edge of Creag na h-Iolaire which means crag of the eagle. After several days of dry weather some boggy pools still remain, around which grow cotton grass and bog asphodel. It is a long, tiring climb on a hot day, and half-way to the cairn seems a good place to picnic.

10

Here a magical moment occurs. From over the top of Meall Mor comes a deep barking noise followed by harsh croaking. Then three birds appear, a pair of ravens mobbing a golden eagle. In time the eagle shakes them off and they retreat to their rocks above Catacol. The eagle, in black silhouette, glides overhead and then, using the thermals to rise over the precipitous edge, it banks into the sun. The sunlight reveals all its patterning and colouring, including its golden neck feathers. It then soars out over the sound, flapping its great wings for the first time. It returns flying overhead once more and then begins to soar in a spiral, up and up, until it can be seen no longer.

Now walk on up the rising slope. Away to the right beyond Catacol Glen lies Lochan a' Mhill (see Walk 4), a bright blue pool among the grassy heights. From the highest point above the crag there are good views in the opposite direction of jagged mountain peaks and, through a V-shape between them, the blue waters of the Sound of Bute. Here several does are disturbed and many footprints and droppings dot the exposed peat. There are red grouse droppings too, but no birds.

Keep well to the left on leaving the cairn and cross a burn on its way to join the Diomhan Burn far below. Then scramble down the long steep hillside through heather and grassy tussocks, always looking ahead for the gentler slopes and the easier way, to the path running through Glen Diomhan. Turn right and

*Eagle*

walk beside the tall deer fence constructed by the Nature Conservancy to protect the service trees. Take the higher path at the end of the fencing. This runs along the slopes below the crags but well above the Catacol Burn in Catacol Glen. This path joins the main path through the glen and after a mile comes to the bridge at Catacol.

This is a rough, adventurous, quiet walk with few paths for much of the way.

*6¹/₂ miles*
*5 hours*

# 2. Catacol, Glen Diomhan, Beinn Tarsuiin, Catacol

Leave the car on the shore side of Catacol Bridge. Here a group of curlews preen and oystercatchers plunge deeply for cockles and worms. Eider duck, large and heavy, fly along the shore just above the waves. Walk up the left side of Catacol Burn for nearly two miles until the entrance to Glen Diomhan is reached. Turn left up the path as it climbs through heather. It runs quite close to the edge of the steep sided ravine through which the lively stream finds its way to join the Catacol. On either side of the narrow path flourish red-topped sphagnum, eyebright and sundew, both round leaved and narrow leaved, with flowers still in bud. Soon the part of the ravine fenced off by the Nature Conservancy is attained. A tall ladder stile gives access to the steep upper slopes of the gorge where both species of service tree, *Sorbus pseudo-fennicus* and *Sorbus Arranensis*, are protected.

*The view from the ridge.*

Continue climbing steadily through Glen Diomhan for two miles. Many gullies run down on either side of the burn and add their waters to the racing Diomhan. In early August the ling is flowering. Butterwort grows and cotton grass blows in the wind. A kestrel hovers over the highest heather-clad slopes hunting for small rodents. As the path rises clubmosses appear. Look back down the glen to the water of the Sound and to the shining surface of Lochan a' Mhill hidden in a hollow on Meall nan Damh.

In time the watershed of the burn is reached and the area is very wet but there are convenient stones to help you across. Beyond, ascend the ridge to an awesome view of Caisteal Abhail and Cir Mhor. Turn right off the ridge and climb up the steep bilberry-covered slopes of Beinn Tarsuiin. Walk along the shoulder to the cairn. On this extensive stony plateau cowberry and cranberry grow where they can. Meadow pipits flit ahead. By a boulder a mass of pipit feathers shows that a sparrow-hawk has been out hunting for food.

From the cairn, at approximately 1,800 feet, the walker can see ridge after ridge of Scotland's great northern mountains in the misty distance. Leave the cairn and walk through the intervening dip to Beinn Tarsuiin's lower top (1,700 feet) keeping well to the left to avoid the marshy watershed of the Calman waterfall. Here ten stags with velvet antlers and rich red coats graze. They stay for some time and then move out of sight. From the top can be

*Stag*

seen the sea around the south west coast of Arran and Kintyre. From this second high point move down the heather and juniper slopes, bearing slightly to the right. The descent goes on and on but the walker is greatly encouraged in his exertions by the sight first of Dubh Loch and then Loch Tanna, silver sheets in their mountain fastness. Look for the cylindrical pale brown droppings left in small piles in grassy clearings among clumps of heather, close to protective boulders. These are evidence of grouse which have fed on heather shoots. Overhead, keeping just above the heather, flies a sparrow-hawk.

When the path beside the Catacol Burn is reached turn right and walk down the glen.

*8 miles*
*6¹/₂ hours*

*Foxglove*

# 3. Catacol, Loch Tanna, Catacol

There is room to park the car by the bridge over the Catacol Burn. Here house martins glide and dive overhead, and a heron flies slowly across the bay. Gorse, a mass of golden blooms, and silver birch grow on the wide shore, a raised beach, left high and dry during glacial times. Oystercatchers probe in the springy green turf.

Walk up the left side of the burn, through foxgloves, tall and pink, and over turf spangled with buttercups and tormentil into Glen Catacol, meaning the ravine of the wild cat. The river is clear and fast-flowing, and it chatters noisily as it hurries on its way over its rocky bed. Close by the water's edge lousewort, milkwort and bog myrtle grow.

On the other side, shaded by birch, a tributary joins the main river. Under young bracken, wood sorrel and wood sage grow. High above, a furious seagull mobs a buzzard that unconcernedly circles, rising ever higher on the air currents.

The energetic may wish to cross the river by the stepping stones and walk over a damp area. They can then climb onto another, higher, raised beach to where heather, sorrel and bluebells flower. A cuckoo calls incessantly from the birch woods behind the cottages at Catacol, and a man cuts grass in long swathes for silage. Hooded crows prod the ground after insects. Far to the left, a waterfall tumbles in a long white slash down the hillside.

Climb down the far side of the raised beach and cross the three channels of the river, or return by the stepping stones, to the north side of the river. Continue walking beside the water until a huge mound of heat-hardened schist is reached. Sit on the mound and enjoy the sun and, in the distance, the bright blue water of Kilbrannon Sound. Look up and see the granite heights above and listen to a curlew calling from the slopes below and a sandpiper piping to its mate along their reach of the river.

Walk along the gently climbing path, parts of which can be wet. It comes close to a waterfall where the burn slides over wide, smooth sloping rocks - sunbathing rocks - beside which grow bog myrtle, lousewort and deep blue milkwort. Look for the beautifully rounded pothole in one of the layers of rock formed by scouring pebbles.

Beside the path, where it begins to climb, orchis, rusty-back fern and hard fern grow, and meadow pipits ascend. In time the path comes to a tributary issuing from Glen Diomhan. Beyond this stream is a barrier of glacial moraine across much of the valley bottom.

The path is now very wet indeed but always passable using strategically-placed boulders. It comes close to the river once more and on the other side a long water-fall leaps impetuously down the steep mountain slopes of Meall nan Damh. At its base it flows over wide rock ledges in a flurry of white foam.

*Sandpiper*

Just beyond this fall the river passes through a gorge and on its steep sides several Arran service trees grow, laden with creamy blossoms. The path hugs the edge of the river and climbs steeply for a quarter of a mile. Below, the water races over smooth rock slides, foam topped at times, but always a lovely blue and very clear.

And then, when a small crest in the path is reached, the spectacular Calman waterfall is revealed beyond. It tumbles, hurtles, plummets from high on the slopes of Beinn Tarsuinn on the left. It drops over wide chunky steps of granite in elegant cascades of white foam. Below this is a very long rock slide, along which the water races with great urgency to join the Catacol Burn.

Beside the fall, in a sun drenched hollow, the walker can picnic and paddle, and explore the river gorge. After a rest continue climbing the path beside the burn, which flows in a flurry of white water in many pretty falls and cascades. For much of its way its bed is wide, flat and very smooth and its banks are beautiful lush gardens, full of various species of fern and heather. Service saplings grow and long stemmed tormentil reaches up through the heather towards the light.

*Loch Tanna*

By the edge of the hurrying water grows sundew, now in delicate white flower. As the path rises, clubmoss and recumbent juniper thrive. Then the watershed of the Catacol Burn is reached. Several feeder streams race downhill draining this very wet area.

Finally a plateau lies ahead, again very wet, and here suddenly the water is flowing in the other direction towards Loch Tanna which lies several hundred yards on. It is the largest loch on the island and lies at 1,100 feet. It is a sparkling sheet of water surrounded by the lower green slopes of the cradling mountains.

*Tormentil*

*8 miles*
*4¹/₂ hours*

# 4. Catacol, Lochan a' Mhill, Catacol

Leave the car on the south side of the bridge over the Catacol Burn. Walk on beside the burn along a good path with bracken on both sides beneath which grow toadstools. A robin scolds from a lower frond, angry at being disturbed in its territory. The path leads to a tributary that races furiously to join the burn. Cross the stream on some large boulders and walk up a bank on the other side to a field which is used for camping and in which stands a large wooden building used by the campers. Turn right along the edge of the field and begin to ascend beside the beck just crossed, passing through high, tedious bracken. Use any small track or sheep trod that makes progress easier.

Along the banks of the stream grow birch, rowan and willow, the haunt of chaffinches, blue tits and wrens. The banks through which the sparkling water dances are colourful with cross-leaved heath, bell heather, ling, marsh thistle and harebells. A small frog hops across a wet patch on the tiny path and bog myrtle, bruised by the walker's boots, gives off a pungent odour.

After a quarter of a mile the bracken gives way to heather and innumerable birch saplings with tiny rowans thriving where they can. House martins circle overhead and wheatears linger on the slopes in late August. Pause regularly and look down to Catacol, surrounded by fields of golden stubble, a view that makes the struggle through the bracken worthwhile.

Keeping the burn to the right, follow the sheep tracks until the bank of a feeder stream is reached. Turn left beside it and walk along a better path that runs next to the little stream through fern, heather, birch saplings and small rowans. Where it passes below some low crags, lousewort and milkwort grow among banks of heather. Ahead, mist veils the top of Meall nan Damh. Behind and below, the Sound of Kilbrannon washes the shores of the Mull of Kintyre, which stretches away to the west.

A slow, gentle half-mile climb leads to a small brow on the skyline and beyond lies the reward of the walk, Lochan a' Mhill, an oblong sheet of water lying in a quiet hollow surrounded by banks of heather. The wind catches the surface of the lochan, stippling the water. From this quiet, unfrequented hollow in the hills issues the small stream which has delighted the walker on the uphill climb.

*Lochan a' Mhill*

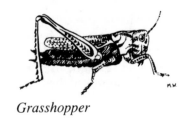

*Grasshopper*

Walk three-quarters of the way round the lochan in an anti-clockwise direction, crossing with care the dozen or more narrow streams running down from the steep slopes of Meall nan Damh. In these, among the sphagnum moss, grow large patches of sundew covered with tall, delicate white flowers. Their red-edged sticky leaves have trapped several minute insects. Then strike up to the ridge of Meall nan Leac Sleamhuinn. Below lies Glen Diomhan and Catacol Glen, with foaming burns racing through the valley bottoms. High on Creag na h-Iolaire stags feed and, as the mist lifts, the jagged top of the Sleeping Warrior is revealed.

Bear left along the ridge following a faint track to the top of the hill ahead. Grasshoppers call and jump in front of the walker. Tiny pools of water reflect the blue sky above and from two closely spaced cairns are glorious views over the sea to mountains in the far distance.

Suddenly a commotion occurs. The writer's dog comes upon several red grouse who cry 'kok, kok, kok' as they are flushed upwards. These red-brown birds, dark-tailed and with curved wings set well back, fly low over the heather and then drop down into the vegetation and are lost to sight. Keeping Catacol in view, climb down the hillside beyond a small burn, which is hastening to swell the Catacol Burn, using sheep trods to help the descent. Towards the lower slopes pass through a wide swathe of heather. Cross the damp area at the foot of the hill, walking through bog myrtle, to reach the large green field seen at the start of the walk.

*Red grouse*

*3 miles*
*3 hours*
*Not to be attempted if the bracken*
*is dense or high*

22

# 5. Mid Thundergay, Coire-Fhionn Lochan, Mid Thundergay

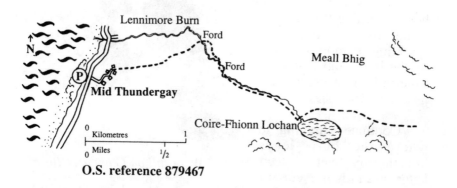

O.S. reference 879467

Leave the car on the verge of the road close to the sea at Mid Thundergay. A signpost directs the way to Coire Lochan. Walk up the cart track, which is lined with flags, early purple orchis, wall pennywort and foxgloves. Pass between the small houses of the hamlet and onto the grassy path where eyebright and buttercups flower. A kissing gate gives access to the open fell and after a hundred yards the path passes through bracken with tormentil below. A deer fence lies ahead and the gate through it is fastened with a quaint iron chain. Over to the left a villager cuts peat and lays it on trestles to dry.

Beyond the deer fence a path leads to the stepping stones that cross the Lennimore Burn. Once across do not walk straight ahead but turn right, following the path until it rejoins the burn

23

(the path takes a diagonal cut across the hillside and the burn descends in a dog-leg). Short heather, cotton grass and bog asphodel soon replace the bracken. Stride across the burn and walk on into a small gorge where the Lennimore descends in two lovely flurries of white water, one after the other, under birch trees where a wren sings loudly. Wood sage and heath overhang the little gorge. In mid afternoon the sun shines into the hollow turning the tumbling water into a myriad of sparkling diamonds. Close by the burn, and below the waterfalls, is a greensward just made for a siesta.

Continue climbing to where the burn leaps impetuously over a steep ledge and falls in a curtain

*Waterfall on Lennimore Burn*

of white water. It is shadowed by more birch, with hard fern and mountain fern, and with tormentil and bell heather close to the water's edge. After another short climb the walker reaches the ridges of rock over which the lively Lennimore cascades, its charm this time unobscured by trees but enhanced, as before, with lush rock gardens on either side. The slopes of Meall Biorach lie to the right and away to the left Meall nan Damh rears up behind Meall Bhig.

The path keeps close to the fast flowing stream and comes to two cairns. Stand here and look back at the blue Sound below, with Kintyre beyond and the Jura mountains spiking the sky. The path very quickly comes to the edge of the lochan, the Lennimore's source. The deep blue Coire-Fhionn Lochan lies in an armchair depression hollowed out by glacial ice. As a dark cloud scuds across the sky the water blackens. The Lochan has three sharp gritty beaches formed of deteriorating granite. The slopes of the semicircular crags on the far side are boulder strewn and steep.

Follow the path along the edge of the lochan where in June pink and mauve violets flower, together with milkwort and butterwort. Continue along the path as it climbs up to the col and look for the tiny lochan on the left, a china-blue colour, reflecting the sky above. The path bears round to the right through short heather and clubmoss. To the east, beyond the intervening valley of the Catacol Burn, lies the Calman waterfall that tumbles down Beinn Tarsuinn seen on Walk 3. Beyond, rear the jagged tops of A'Chir and Cir Mhor. Then, at the head of Glen Catacol, to the walker's right, lies Loch Tanna, long and slim, and a sparkling blue in the warm afternoon sun.

*4¹/₂ miles*
*2¹/₂ hours*

*Coire-Fhionn Lochan*

# 6. Pirnmill, lochan in Glas Choirein below Beinn Bharrain, Pirnmill

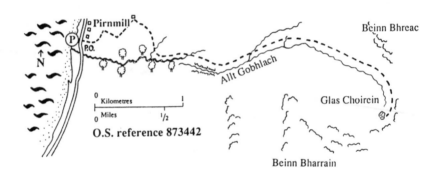

O.S. reference 873442

Park on a grass verge on the shore side of the road, fifty yards north of the bridge over the Allt Gobhlach and the Pirnmill Post Office. Walk up the track opposite, thereby avoiding the very wet path beside the Gobhlach behind the post office. Continue on the track for half a mile then, when the last house on the track comes into view, strike diagonally to the right over a lovely slope of low-growing summer flowers. Here blooms the delicate field felwort, a pretty mauve gentian. After climbing the slope join a track that continues to the right into a small birch wood. Cross a tiny stream hurrying through flags, marsh woundwort and wild mint. Continue along the path through the trees to more open ground and take a stile over a wire fence. This leads to a path and to a tall ladder stile in the deer fence. Here three young speckled robins remain perched on the wire fence much to the consternation of the parent robin, which bobs from post to post 'ticking' anxiously.

Beyond the deer fence lies the open moor. Pause and look back to the glorious view of the Sound below and Kintyre beyond. Ahead and to the right lies a steep-sided ravine lined with birch, oak and aspen and beneath the trees races the white-topped Allt Gobhlach. The sides of the ravine, a glorious mountain garden, are clad with various species of fern, heather, bilberry and golden rod. Walk on for half a mile along the side of the burn to where the stream, which issues out of Coire Roinn, tumbles in three spectacular waterfalls to add its water to the Gobhlach.

Keep to the north bank of the burn until reaching the last of the birches cradling the raging water. Follow a well worn path down to the burn and clamber over on convenient boulders. Cross over a tongue of moor to the side of a tributary that drains from Glas Choirein. The banks of the burn are covered with lush vegetation in striking contrast to the bleak moorland all around. In parts the bed of the burn is composed of smooth sheets of granite over which the water slides fast and clear. Wheatears and meadow pipits abound. Grasshoppers chirrup and the air seems overfull of daddy-long-legs. Cross the burn. To the right looms the large mass of Beinn Bharrain with its scree slopes, crags and coires.

*Beinn Bharrain*

27

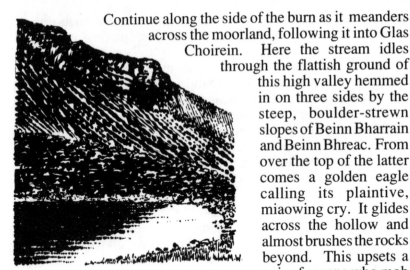
*Lochan in Glas Choirein*

Continue along the side of the burn as it meanders across the moorland, following it into Glas Choirein. Here the stream idles through the flattish ground of this high valley hemmed in on three sides by the steep, boulder-strewn slopes of Beinn Bharrain and Beinn Bhreac. From over the top of the latter comes a golden eagle calling its plaintive, miaowing cry. It glides across the hollow and almost brushes the rocks beyond. This upsets a pair of ravens who mob it until it flies out over the Sound. Once over the water it soars and glides for at least five minutes and then it returns, joined by its mate. As the pair circle the tops, the ravens start to mob once more and in time the eagles glide away over the mountain.

Ahead, at the blind end of the hollow, a herd of stags turns nervously and watches our approach. As we continue towards them the animals begin to move out of their trap. A large stag, with a regal tracery of antlers, leads the way, followed by all the others in an orderly line, with the smallest bringing up the rear. They pass within sixty feet of the invaders of their privacy and then head out onto the open moor. As they pass a small coire high up under the jagged top of a ridge of Beinn Bharrain, a small herd of stags files down and joins the larger group.

Grouse droppings occur in sheltered hollows among the heather but the birds are nowhere to be seen. A curlew's apology for a nest lies close by, its three large oval eggs at first appearing intact, but each has a minute hole through which the contents have been sucked. The dog, enjoying the scent of the deer, is called, and a double echo of her name comes ringing back.

Now the sun-filled coire is silent.  Continue ascending gently, bearing slightly to the right to a small eminence at the head of the coire.  Beyond this lies the tiny lochan, a shallow pool bedded with flat, smooth boulders, reflecting the austere outline of the peaks above.  Small green rosettes, the leaves of lobelia, grow among the boulders beneath the water.  Look back to the Sound and Kintyre and to the Sound of Gigha and the island itself. Further into the distance lie the Sound and mountains of Jura and the mountains of Islay.  On the far horizon one can see the uplands of the Island of Mull.

*5 miles*
*5 hours*

# 7. The Caves and Shoreline at Imachar

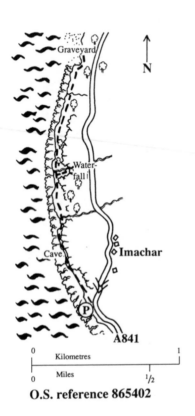

O.S. reference 865402

If driving from the direction of Pirnmill, park on the shore at the bottom of the steepish hill beyond Imachar. A grassy track leads along the shore towards the Imachar cliffs. The shore is very rocky and during a south-west gale the waves crash in and spray flies into the air. Eiders bob up and down on the waves and gannets dive in their own spectacular way.

Climb the gate in a wire fence, bordered with flags, and walk on past a huge crag, bright purple with bell heather. The shore, a raised beach, is grassy here and the cliffs stand back and are covered with rowan, willow, sycamore and ivy. In a tangle of bramble and bracken a robin 'tics' as it is disturbed.

As you walk along, the cliffs become even higher and are covered with thrift, harebells, yarrow, foxgloves, spearwort, self-heal, ragwort and a grey-green lichen.

*Eiders*

Below the towering cliffs the first cave is seen. It is a shallow, sheltered cavern much favoured by sheep. On the steep faces above, wall pennywort, sea campion and thrift grow in every possible crevice. Nearby, another cave stretches deep into the rock with burdock and silver weed flourishing at the entrance.

Continue along the path, which is easy to follow. On either side tormentil, self-heal, foxgloves, yarrow, thyme, harebells, pink clover, common stonecrop, tufted vetch, ragwort and yellow bedstraw cover the turf with a riot of colour. Honeysuckle climbs over the lower slopes of the cliffs.

When a fence across the beach is reached, and the tide is in, climb some easy rocks on the left to reach the lovely, wide, secluded, grassy sward ahead. Here the cliffs stand even further back and are covered with rowan, birch and hazel. The turf of this raised beach is spangled with thyme, harebells, pink clover, sea campion, hawkweed, pink eyebright, tormentil, common stonecrop, scurvy

*Cave at Imachar*

31

grass, yellow rattle, yellow bedstraw and yarrow. Just beyond the little stream that crosses this stretch, turn right and walk through bracken and flags along a narrow path, where a wren sings a sweet song. The path passes behind a huge boulder where more honeysuckle perfumes the air. Recross the stream and from this side a marvellous view is obtained of a spectacular waterfall. The stream tumbles down the cliff in one long jet onto some projecting rocks, then bounces off to cascade into a deep pool. Behind the lace-like water, liverworts and fern thrive, and around the pool purple loosestrife and cat's valerian flower.

Return to the path and look for the tiny rose saplings that cover an extensive area. One plant has a small hip on it.

*Second waterfall at Imachar*

Towards the end of this part of the beach another, even longer, waterfall comes leaping exultantly from the cliff top, dropping into a small copse of hazel, birch, rowan, willow and honeysuckle. It falls in a long wall of white water, then spreads fan-like into a deep pool. In the cliffs on either side, several small caves are hidden behind the bracken.

Follow the path over a wet area and look here for the beautiful grass of Parnassus flowering between ragged robin, bog asphodel, orchis and bog myrtle. To the right another waterfall descends. Just after this marshy area, a beach covered with large round boulders stretches ahead. The path avoids these by moving into the trees and comes to a little burial ground surrounded by a low wall. Among the flags, meadow sweet, woundwort and ferns that grow tall inside, and where a robin sings, are gravestones bearing inscriptions to many of the McMillen family.

Return along the same paths. This is doubly pleasurable because there is so much to see that was missed on the outward walk.

*3 miles*
*2¹/₂ hours*

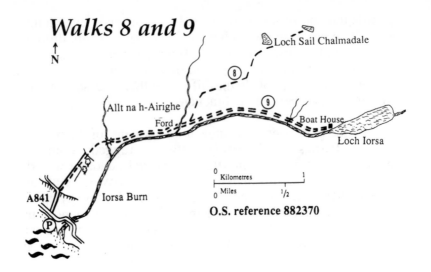

Loch Sail Chalmadale

⑧

Allt na h-Airighe

Ford

⑨

Boat House

Loch Iorsa

A841    Iorsa Burn

P

0
Kilometres          1

0  Miles          ½

**O.S. reference 882370**

# 8. Dougarie, two lochans below Sail Chalmadale, Dougarie

When travelling north from Blackwaterfoot look for the wide grassy parking area on the shore just beyond the bridge over the Iorsa Burn. Immediately opposite, a cart track leads to a farm. Walk along this. Where it swings to the left look for a signposted footpath, through long grass, that climbs the cliff of a raised beach. Here the charming marsh woundwort grows, together with ragwort and meadow sweet. At the top of the 'stranded' cliff climb the stile, following the directions on a signpost which tell you to follow the wall for all its length. Climb the low fence at the end of the wall into a small wood of sycamores and limes. A ladder stile gives access to a path beyond the trees and then passes through bracken and gorse. Black and white marker posts showing clearly among the vegetation guide the walker through the lush greenery.

Pass through a gate and follow the path as it climbs a heathery slope and then drops down to a bridge across the Allt na h-Airighe. On a fence, mink with all shades of fur, and several hoodies, fill a game keeper's larder. Once across the bridge the path joins a wide cart track, richly bordered with heather, that swings out into the U-shaped valley. To the right flows the Iorsa, wide and surging, the water racing round the many boulders scattered over its bed. In places bog myrtle grows and scrub willow, too. Ragwort, not kept under control by the cinnibar caterpillar, grows riotously and this brightly-coloured weed contrasts strikingly with the flowering heather. Walk through the next gate and then cross the burn (which comes down from Glen Scaftigill) on large, conveniently placed stepping stones.

Once over the burn look for a narrow path on the left that leaves the main track and winds up the ridge towards the lochans and Sail Chalmadale. The path, which is easy to miss, strikes off at the edge of the bracken that borders the burn and follows beside the racing water for fifty yards. To pinpoint the beginning of the path, look for six posts

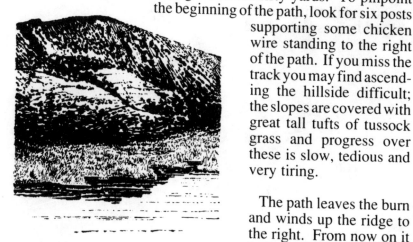

supporting some chicken wire standing to the right of the path. If you miss the track you may find ascending the hillside difficult; the slopes are covered with great tall tufts of tussock grass and progress over these is slow, tedious and very tiring.

The path leaves the burn and winds up the ridge to the right. From now on it is distinct and easy to walk along. Bordered by heather and grass, it cuts deeply

*The first of the two lochans.*

into the peaty underlying soil, trodden down by the feet of humans and innumerable deer. It leads, after three-quarters of a mile, to the first lochan, a quiet tranquil stretch of water. From here a path leads directly to the slopes of Sail Chalmadale, with a good climb ahead.

*Oak eggar moth*
*caterpillar on*
*heather*

The second lochan, a smaller peaty pool surrounded by reeds, lies three hundred yards to the right of the first. It is on slightly higher ground and so cannot be seen from the first. Meadow pipits, having reared their young, fly over the moor below the mountain and oak eggar moth caterpillars, enjoying the heather, sometimes venture across the path.

An exhilarating walk with splendid views and solitude.

*5 miles*
*2¹/₂ hours*

# 9. Dougarie, Loch Iorsa, Dougarie

Leave the car and walk to the stepping stones as for the walk to the two lochans below Sail Chalmadale (Walk 8). If the burn is in spate, then it is off with boots and socks. The track continues for half a mile. A pair of ravens dive acrobatically over the edge of a crag on Beinn Lochain. Several does appear on the skyline of Creag a' Chromain.

The track ends just beyond the weir and by the boathouse. Ahead lies Loch Iorsa, purled by the wind, a dull grey expanse of water reflecting a dark cloud above. On the far side a dozen common gulls preen on the shore, protected by overhanging clumps of heather and grass from a chill wind 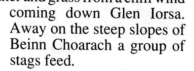 coming down Glen Iorsa. Away on the steep slopes of Beinn Choarach a group of stags feed.

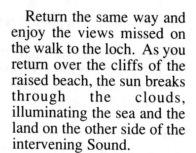 Return the same way and enjoy the views missed on the walk to the loch. As you return over the cliffs of the raised beach, the sun breaks through the clouds, illuminating the sea and the land on the other side of the intervening Sound.

*Loch Iorsa*

*4 miles*
*2 hours*

# 10. Auchencar Druid's Stone

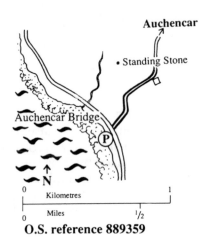

Auchencar

• Standing Stone

Auchencar Bridge

P

N

0  Kilometres  1

0  Miles  ¹/₂

**O.S. reference 889359**

Auchencar means the field of rocky land. The signpost to Auchencar lies between Machrie and Dougarie. Park on the grassy flat that edges the shore and look towards Auchencar to where the Druid's Stone stands in the middle of a field, stark, white and spectacular. Walk along the metalled road beside the field, where you are closer to the megalith, clearly visible in the pasture full of sheep. There seems to be no public right of way to the stone, but the view from the road is so good that one is not tempted to trespass.

Return to the car and enjoy the birds on this lovely, quiet stretch of shore. Gannets, from Ailsa Craig, rise high above the waves before diving into the sea for fish. Eider, in small family groups, float a little off shore, the male resplendent in black and white plumage leading the line. Red-throated divers swim low in the water, their long thin necks pointed upwards. They dive suddenly and are lost to sight among the waves. Oystercatchers doze on large boulders or, in pairs, probe the mud. Several handsome shelduck hunt for worms and tiny crabs, occasionally racing over the sandy shore after sand-hoppers. Nearby a raft of sixty to seventy red-breasted mergansers move as one, first one way and then the other, sometimes in a long line, sometimes in a very close-knit mass. Not until they reach the shelter of some convenient boulders do they abandon the orderly grouping and move apart to feed with heads just below the surface.

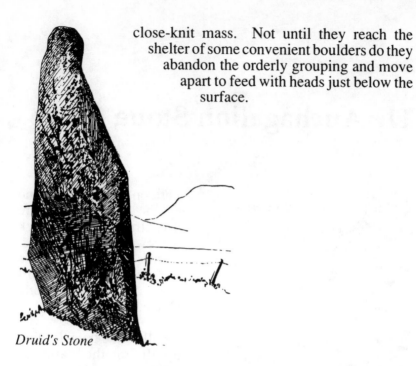

*Druid's Stone*

*¹/₂ mile*
*10 minutes*

# 11. Auchagallon Stone Circle

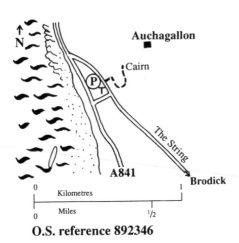

**Auchagallon**

**Cairn**

P

N

**The String**

**A841**

**Brodick**

0     Kilometres     1

0     Miles     ¹/₂

**O.S. reference 892346**

Park on the corner of land by the phone box where The String road to Brodick leaves the shore road. Across the road is the ancient monument signpost to Auchagallon Stone Circle.

Follow the track leading uphill to the farm at Auchagallon. On either side grow harebells, wood sage, scabious, hawkweed, heather, yarrow and pink and white clover. Two hundred yards ahead lies the circle of red sandstone slabs, forty-seven feet in diameter with fifteen stones surviving. Within

*Auchagallon Stone Circle*

the circle are the remains of a burial cairn under which a stone cist was found dating from the Bronze Age, possibly between 1800 and 1400 B.C.

On the mound within and outside the circle of stones, harebells, ragwort, yarrow, hawkbit, clover, sorrel, plantain, scabious and many grasses thrive. Overhead a heron flies towards the shore, head drawn back and long legs trailing.

*Heron*

*250 yards*
*20 minutes*

# 12. Machrie Farm, Cnoc na Ceille, Machrie Farm

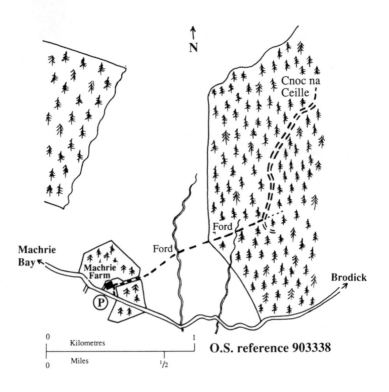

O.S. reference 903338

Leave the car on the grass verge by Machrie Farm. Take the first turn that leads into the farm and then follow the track as it bears to the right and climbs uphill. This is the start of an old cart track. In just under a mile the new Forestry Commission road is reached.

Turn to the left passing through the gate across the road. Beyond lie extensive plantings of conifers by the Commission. Follow the substantial dirt road, with its red sandstone hard core, into the heart of this very young forest. Plants have barely started to colonise the verges of the track but the spruce and rowan saplings thrive well. In the small crevices among boulders flanking the road eyebright, buttercup, sneezewort, harebell, tormentil and bog myrtle grow. Meadow pipits fly low over the small trees and herring gulls wing towards the sea. To the north lie the bleak slopes of Beinn Bharrain.

*Buttercup*

When the road comes to an abrupt end, after a mile and a quarter, continue uphill along a wide grassy track, with heather growing on either side, to the top of the little hill, Cnoc na Ceille. From here one can look down on the thousands of immature trees and on hillside after hillside herring-boned with dykes. Below lies Machrie Farm almost encircled by small conifers. In great contrast to the new conifers, a fine row of Scots pine, planted many years ago, acts as a wind break for the farm. Beyond lie the grey waters of the sound, reflecting the storm clouds above.

The crest of the little hill is covered with soft yellow grass blown hither and thither in the wind. Heather blooms and cowberry, growing between, is covered with red, acid berries.

*3 miles*
*1¹/₂ hours*

*Harebell*

# 13. Moss Farm Road Stone Circle and Machrie Moor Stone Circles

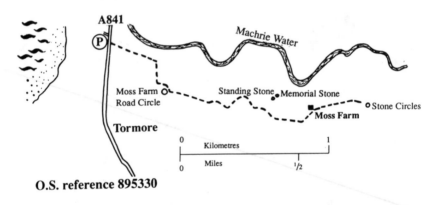

**A841**

Machrie Water

Moss Farm Road Circle

Standing Stone   Memorial Stone

Stone Circles

**Moss Farm**

**Tormore**

| 0 | Kilometres | 1 |
| 0 | Miles | 1/2 |

**O.S. reference 895330**

Stone circles may have been constructed for religious reasons, perhaps as calendars using the position of the sun and moon, or as meeting places, but no one can be quite sure why they were built.

To reach the circles park in a small place opposite the ancient monument sign. There is room for only three or four vehicles. The sign directs the walker to the circles - half a mile to Moss Farm Road Circle and one and a half miles to the Machrie Moor Stone Circles.

*Curlew*

44

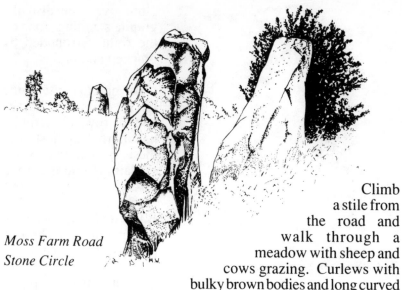

*Moss Farm Road*
*Stone Circle*

Climb a stile from the road and walk through a meadow with sheep and cows grazing. Curlews with bulky brown bodies and long curved beaks fly overhead with wild whistles. To the left the wide, brown, fast-flowing Machrie Water races beneath birch and ash, with bracken and tufted vetch below.

The cart track swings to the right to a broken gate beyond which lies the Moss Farm Road Circle. Within a single row of granite boulders are the scanty remains of a burial cairn. The latter dates from the Bronze Age, 2000 - 1500 B.C., but the stone circle may be a little earlier.

Continue along the track, which now passes through open moorland with pasture away to the left. Juncus, heather, orchis and bog asphodel compete with purple moor grass.

Just before the next stile notice the standing stone to the left and the m o d e r n monument

*Machrie Moor Stone Circle*

45

*Red sandstone slab*

close by. See also the granite standing stone on the right surrounded by bracken and orchis.

Beyond the stile to the left lie derelict buildings and a row of scrubby hawthorn, and just past these is a notice board explaining that the stone circles were erected between 1800 and 1400 B.C. and that various implements and a bronze pin have been found.

Young meadow pipits frequent the moorland and a fledgling wheatear with short tail feathers flutters from one clump of vegetation to the next. Overhead common gulls wheel and circle, and a lesser black-back gull wings its way to the shore.

The first circle beyond the notice board is a double one, formed of large granite stones and from this circle one can see almost all the other circles and standing stones. Away to the left one spectacular red sandstone slab stands grandly, with several lying on the ground around it. Further on, in another sandstone circle, three splendid stones stand proudly. Two more circles to the right, constructed of granite, have been partly excavated.

Linger awhile among the stones and think back in time. The surrounding hills, quiet and mist topped, must have appeared much the same when the stones were put in place.

*3 miles*
*2 hours*

46

# 14. King's Cave from Machrie

There is a wide grass verge just to the south of Ashlar Farm, Machrie, on the right hand side of the road for those travelling from the north. This verge is just beyond the post box on the left and the signposted cart track. Close by the farm, swallows and starlings sit on overhead wires, and house martins wheel across the fields where cattle graze.

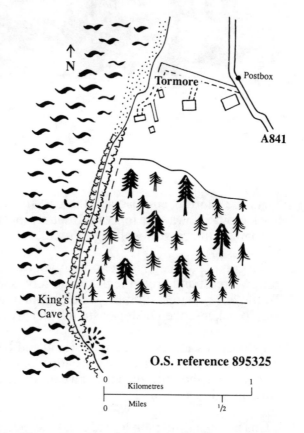

O.S. reference 895325

Follow the cart track towards Tormore and the shore. It is bordered with ragwort, hawkweed, harebells, knapweed, yarrow, pink clover, tufted vetch and hogweed, the latter giving off a strong, rank smell. A young robin, still with its speckled breast, hops about a hawthorn bush.

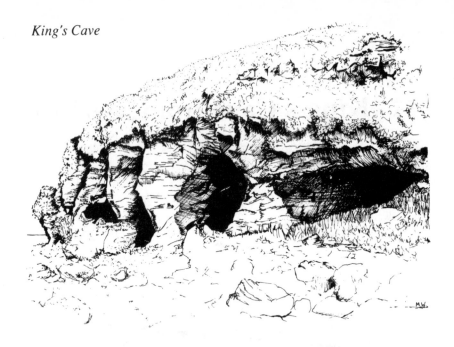

As the shore is approached, the cart track swings to the left. Rock pipits sit on a wire fence and then fly towards the shore. Here the path to the cave is well signposted.

The grassy path begins to climb. A young willow warbler, with yellow breast and brown legs, plaintively 'kweets' from a bush. To the left are great clumps of bell heather and ling, and to the right bracken-covered slopes stretch steeply downwards.

A stile gives access to open moorland and 100 yards on another stile leads into a Forestry Commission wood planted with spruce. Just beyond the stile meadow sweet, angelica, and brooklime grow in a tiny stream.

This is a beautiful path to walk and the views across the placid, clear waters of the Sound to Kintyre are superb. But take care on the muddy parts.

Below, an eider drake is closely followed by two rotund ducks.

The tide is slowly ebbing, and the rocks can be seen through the blue water. A pack of mergansers float idly in the sunshine, preening perfunctorily, and then appear to snooze, drifting along with the tide, but still keeping close. A wren sings strongly, concealed in a thicket.

After a mile the path begins to drop and becomes drier. Look for a hidden ravine running down to the shore that has water flowing along it. One can pass through dryshod using the stepped rocks.

On the left, at the bottom of the cleft, water runs off the cliff above and falls in a wide sheet of drips into a pool, forming a natural grotto. Here liverworts thrive together with moneywort. Overhead a pair of fulmars make huge arcs, catching the wind as they fly from their ledge on the cliffs.

The path reaches the shingle, where grow thrift, sea campion, herb robert and silver weed. Another young willow warbler, again quite yellow, calls from a bush at the bottom of the cliff. Rock pipits abound. The air is full of summer sounds as bees and various insects flit from heather-covered cliffs across the shore.

The caves in the red sandstone lie ahead, set well back from the high tide line. King's Cave, named after Robert the Bruce, has iron gates but these are open and one can walk into the high topped cavern. Straight ahead is a large bluff of rock with two blind-ended tunnels, one on either side. It is on this bluff, or buttress of rock, that faint carvings, possibly dating from early Christian or Viking times, can be discerned. One is of a large cross standing in some sort of vegetation. The other, to

*Carving on cave wall*

the right, towards the top of the cross, is of a human figure holding, perhaps, a bow above its head. The cave may have been used as a chapel in the fifth century A.D. Meetings of the Kirk Session were held here in the eighteenth century.

*Fulmars*

On a ledge above the cave a pair of fulmars 'ek,ek,ek' to each other among the thrift and sorrel. The next cave has two small caves above, and beyond are several smaller caves, dark ovals in the yellow red sandstone, with interesting layers of strata towards the top.

Returning, enjoy the view of Beinn Bharrain ahead with Beinn Tarsuiin to its right.

*4 miles*
*2 hours*

# 15. King's Cave from Blackwaterfoot

Use the public parking by the golf course at Blackwaterfoot. This is approached by a right turn at the bottom of the hill before the road runs along the shore towards the harbour by the Kinloch Hotel. The golf course is well signposted.

Walk to the shore and continue west along the sand. To the right, the small sand dunes are covered with marram

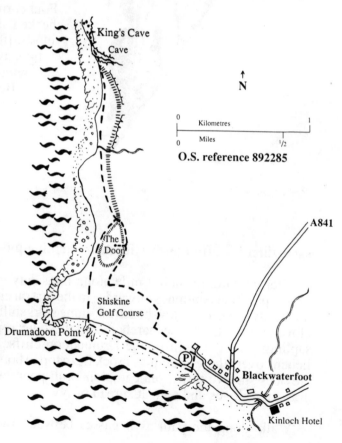

King's Cave

Cave

N

0       Kilometres       1

0       Miles       1/2

**O.S. reference 892285**

A841

The Doon

Shiskine Golf Course

Drumadoon Point

P

**Blackwaterfoot**

Kinloch Hotel

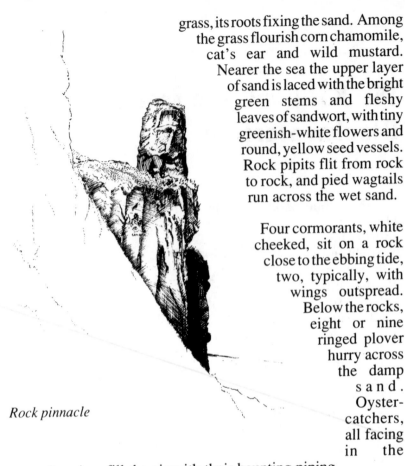

grass, its roots fixing the sand. Among the grass flourish corn chamomile, cat's ear and wild mustard. Nearer the sea the upper layer of sand is laced with the bright green stems and fleshy leaves of sandwort, with tiny greenish-white flowers and round, yellow seed vessels. Rock pipits flit from rock to rock, and pied wagtails run across the wet sand.

Four cormorants, white cheeked, sit on a rock close to the ebbing tide, two, typically, with wings outspread. Below the rocks, eight or nine ringed plover hurry across the damp sand. Oyster-catchers, all facing in the

*Rock pinnacle*

same direction, fill the air with their haunting piping.

After walking for half a mile along the sandy beach follow a grassy path that continues onwards. In the turf on either side grow thrift, silver weed, yellow bedstraw, dune storksbill, yarrow, pink clover, tormentil, thyme, harebells, vetch, stonecrop and tiny rose saplings. To the right lie the Drumadoon cliffs. Bluish-green lichen covers these columns of rock from top to bottom, and in the crevices survive thrift, sea campion, wall pennywort, bleached grass, foxgloves and a great spread of ivy.

Walk along the path as it passes between two huge rocky

outcrops, crossing the farthest tip of the golf course. Climb a stile in the fence, turning right to walk uphill towards the rock pinnacle seen so clearly from either direction when travelling on the coast road. The path then bears north at the base of the spectacular columnar cliffs, well above the seashore. From this high path, King's Cave and the smaller caves nearby can be seen across the bay, a mile or so ahead, with Beinn Bharrain, tall and sombre beyond.

Innumerable flowers border this path. Here grow harebells, yellow bedstraw, self heal, thyme, stonecrop, tormentil, foxgloves, daisies and valerian. Where the ground is damp purple loosestrife, meadow sweet, brooklime and St. John's wort flourish. A stumpy tailed wren, with rufous brown feathers, flits from bracken top to foxglove, singing as it goes. A fulmar flies with few wing beats along the cliff face.

Where the path drops down a little towards the shore, burdock, hawthorn, blackthorn, ivy, bramble, ragwort, wood sage, polypody fern and forget-me-nots thrive. At the end of the columns, the path is joined by another coming from the cliff top, and then leads down to a wide, grassy, raised beach. Wheatears and wagtails seem ever present. Away to the left among the rocks more oystercatchers consort with curlews, all seeming to enjoy the sun, but protected by the rocks from the breeze coming off the water. On one of these rocks stands a dotterel.

The path crosses the raised beach for another half mile and then

*King's Cave*

53

climbs between red sandstone to the caves beyond. (For what to look for in the King's Cave see previous walk). The shingle beach outside the caves is protected from the offsea breeze and, in the full sun, is just the place for an afternoon siesta.

Return along the grassy path over the raised beach and take the steep path that climbs left to the top of the cliffs. At the top, walk to a gate on the right and then climb onto what was, possibly, the ramparts of a large Iron Age fort, giving refuge to a tribal community. Follow an indistinct path through bracken to a stile and then continue on, past more bracken and flags, to a gate into the site of the fort. A path through the grass leads to one rather forlorn standing stone but behind it is a marvellous view of the northern peaks. The huge mound is covered with flowering grasses, harebells and tormentil and away by the cliff edge grows the ubiquitous bracken. It must have been a wonderful site for observing invaders but a very windy one at times.

Return back to the gate and turn right, walking along the ramparts of the fort. Eventually the path drops through bracken to a field and a gate in the right-hand corner. Turn left and walk along the edge of the golf course. To the left grows a field of barley and, at its edge, corn marigold, white dead nettle, bugloss, red goosefoot and pink persicaria. When a farm cart track is reached turn right and follow it back to the car.

*5 miles*
*3 hours*

*Pinnacle seen on return from cave*

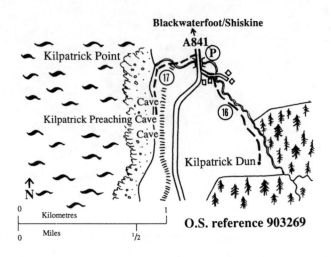

Blackwaterfoot/Shiskine

A841

Kilpatrick Point

Cave

Kilpatrick Preaching Cave

Cave

Kilpatrick Dun

0 Kilometres 1

0 Miles ¹/₂

**O.S. reference 903269**

# 16. Kilpatrick Dun

Park just before a small bridge over the stream at Kilpatrick if approaching from Shiskine or Blackwaterfoot. Leave the car on the left hand side of the road close to the low wall of a farm. Turn left into a farm track as directed by an ancient monument sign. After twenty yards an arrow on a black and white post directs the walker to the right down a lane leading to a gate and a stile. Along this lane grow yarrow tinged with pink, harebells, foxgloves and bramble in blossom. Curlews call as they fly overhead. Beyond the stile the way is indistinct and the walker needs to look for black and white posts marching up the hillside. The route lies close to a small burn which idles its way between thickly wooded banks where willow, hawthorn, rowan, ash and birch shade the water.

The way becomes very wet and muddy where the cattle have trodden but as the path climbs the heather-clad hillside, it becomes drier. After a half mile uphill Kilpatrick Dun lies ahead.

*Kilpatrick Dun*

The ancient monument notice explains that the 'cashel', or wall, is built of stone and earth and encloses an area of three acres. The focal point of the cashel is the dun, a ruined circular drystone homestead that lies on the northern side. A number of chambers are set within the thickness of the wall and several hut circles lie outside the cashel. The monument dates possibly from the beginning of the Christian era.

What a marvellous site these early folk chose. They, too, must have enjoyed the summer sea below, blue and sparkling. Across the water they would have seen Kintyre, and Ireland in the distance, and away to the north the large mass of Beinn Bharrain.

Today the dun overlooks cultivated fields that stretch to Blackwaterfoot. On all other sides the Forestry Commission's trees encroach. The stones have stood for hundreds of years and from one near the centre of the site the walker can see the stone circles on Machrie Moor.

*2 miles*
*1 hour*

56

# 17. Kilpatrick Cave

Park as for Kilpatrick Dun (see Walk 16). Cross the road and pass through a gate on the north side of the stream. Follow a wide grassy area between scrubby hawthorns and bordered with foxgloves and harebells to where the beck swings across the path. Sheep graze to the left and barley and oats grow in a pasture to the right.

Wade or step across the burn and walk on to a gate in the fence on the edge of the shore. Here oystercatchers and curlews call, and hooded crows, starlings and pied wagtails quarter the beach for tasty morsels. Turn left and walk along a springy turf path that runs just above the pebbled beach. Here on either side grow buttercups, thistles, spearwort, yarrow and yellow bedstraw. Rabbits scuttle up the low cliffs on the left and a wheatear flits ahead.

*Pied wagtail*

After a quarter of a mile the cliffs are higher and under great rocky overhangs are several caves. One small cave has a smaller one above it. Then comes Kilpatrick Cave, named after the hermit Patrick. This was once used as the parish school and also for religious services. In the nineteenth century it was used as a meeting place for those fanatics who wanted a fervent priest to replace the

57

milder man presented by the 9th Duke of Hamilton. Around the cave grow dense bracken, golden rod and ling, and among the pebbles flourish pink persicaria, burdock and sorrel.

*Kilpatrick Cave*

*1 mile*
*1 hour*

# 18.  Corriecravie Shore, Torr a' Chaisteil, Corriecravie

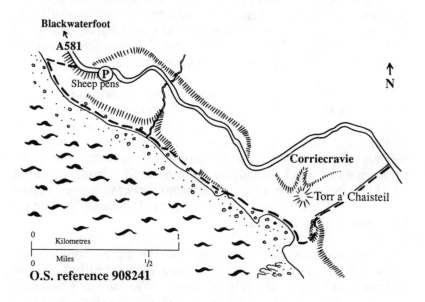

**Blackwaterfoot**

**A581**

**P**

**Sheep pens**

**N**

**Corriecravie**

**Torr a' Chaisteil**

0    Kilometres    1

0    Miles    ¹/₂

**O.S. reference 908241**

Two and a half miles south of Blackwaterfoot, where the coast road leaves the cliff edge and moves inland, look for a parking verge by some sheep pens on the shore side of the road.  Walk back fifty yards to an overgrown cart track that runs down to the shore and is shown on the O.S. map at 908241.  Close by the verge, on a post supporting an overhead power line, sits a merlin with streaked and mottled under-parts and tinged with red, denoting its

*Merlin*

59

immaturity. This small raptor calls 'kiek, kiek, kiek, kiek' plaintively, and then flies towards the shore. After a few minutes it returns to its post.

Walk down the grassy track lined with summer flowers. By-pass the wet areas, using convenient stones, and cross a low wire fence to reach the shore. Curlews feed on the ebbing tide and fill the air with their bubbling calls. Turn left and follow an indistinct grassy path between boulders below the scattered dwellings of Corriecravie on the cliffs above. Here on the shore grow a wonderful variety of summer flowers including yellow bedstraw, silver weed, thrift, yarrow, corn chamomile, skull cap, stonecrop, purple loosestrife, honeysuckle, wild thyme, knapweed and lousewort. Earlier in the year a mass of yellow flags flowered but now only the long, oval seed boxes remain.

After a hundred yards the path becomes wider and easier to follow. At the water's edge lesser black-back gulls and eider feed, several shags crowd on a rock and a cormorant flies northwards. Further out, on more rocks, common seals bask and wriggle round to watch the walker pass along the shore. Wheatears flit from rock to rock, one flying up into the air, adroitly catching a luckless insect. Butterflies flutter from flower to flower. A pair of whinchats cling to the top of bracken stalks constantly fanning their tails as they call quietly.

At times the path continues away from the shore through dense bracken but always in the direction of the Dun or hill-fort. As the soft sea mist lifts, Ailsa Craig looms up. When a wire fence bars the way ahead, turn right and walk down to the shore to skirt a small bay. By now the singularly shaped fort can be seen clearly away to the left. Look for a gate in the fence on the left that gives access to a path leading across the pasture to the base of the Dun. Sitting on a wire strand of the fence is a male stonechat with conspicuous black head, white about its neck and a warm rufous red breast.

The ancient monument sign stands on the far side of the fort. Torr a' Chaisteil, Corriecravie, consists of a single rampart wall enclosing a circle about forty-five feet in diameter with an entry

*Torr a' Chaisteil*

on the east side. Its builders must have spent many years and much labour in its construction. It has been excavated on several occasions but the only objects known to have been found are some animal bones and the top stone of a hand mill. Archaeologists believe the fort to have been constructed in the early centuries A.D. From the top the walker has a splendid view over the small bays along the shore and the surrounding land - no doubt the reason the fort was constructed here. It also makes an ideal place for a picnic.

From the fort a signposted track returns to the road. But the seals are very engaging and the walker might return instead along the lovely quiet deserted shore once more.

*4 miles*
*2¹/₂ hours*

# Walk 19

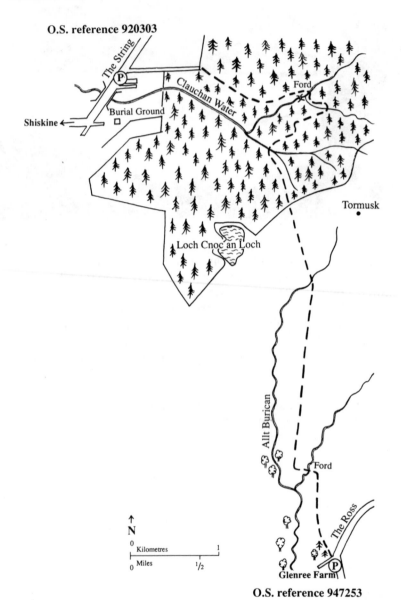

O.S. reference 920303

The String

P

Clauchan Water

Ford

Burial Ground

Shiskine ←

Tormusk

Loch Cnoc an Loch

Allt Burican

Ford

The Ross

↑
N

0 Kilometres 1

0 Miles ½

Glenree Farm

P

O.S. reference 947253

# 19. Glenree to Shiskine

Two cars are needed for this walk, one parked by the gates to the burial ground north of Shiskine and the second left at the start of the walk at Glenree, towards the south end of The Ross road. At a bend where The Ross swings sharply to the right, the road to Glenree Farm turns off to the left. The track where the walk starts runs straight ahead beyond a gate.

To the left of the path a jay wings through a small beech wood and to the right sheep graze. Swallows and house martins wheel overhead in the warmth of a late July day. Soon the trees are left behind and the rather indistinct path leads to a gate in a wire fence. Once through, head for another gate on the opposite side of the pasture. Here hooded crows probe for insects in the turf, meadow brown butterflies flit among the flowers and toadstools flourish in the cow pats.

*Jay*

After the gate turn left and walk through the bracken to an alder copse beside the Burican Burn. Cross the brown, peat-stained stream by convenient stones and immediately climb a heather slope to a path bearing slightly to the right through bracken, foxgloves and harebells, keeping in sound of the burn. The path leads out of the bracken into heather that covers an exposed tongue of land between two tributaries of the Burican. It is this tongue of land that should be kept in sight in order to find the way across from Glenree.

Follow the path which climbs steadily up the moorland slope. In a drainage ditch running beside the path grow scrub willow, bog stitchwort, tormentil, hard fern, marsh thistle, milkmaids and several species of rush. To the west the land sweeps downwards in a cloud of cotton grass to the burn, and to the east are the slopes of Tormusk with its cairn on top. Meadow pipits flit ahead and then turn and fly very close, anxious for their young still fluttering unsurely from one clump of heather to the next. Look back regularly to the blue waters of the Sound far down below, with the green slopes of Kintyre beyond. Soon the path passes through a vast expanse of heath and heather towards a gate and a stile into the forest. Just before the walker reaches the forest fence, he is surprised by a glorious view. Over the top of the trees the Sound, Kintyre and the mountains of Jura can be seen.

The path through the forest, bordered by bracken, foxgloves, climbing corydalis, tormentil and bedstraw, passes between many acres of immature spruce. After nearly a mile the path comes to an open area free of trees and then zig-zags down a steep slope to the Clauchan Glen and Burn. Lime was once quarried beside the first zig-zag and now a wonderful variety of flowers proliferate. Wild strawberries grow in profusion and provide succulent refreshment.

Wild raspberries flourish, with common speedwell, lady's mantle, water avens, primroses and violets.

*Primrose*

64

Cross the fast-flowing Clauchan by boulders or, lower downstream, by a rickety wooden bridge, and continue along the path as it climbs the other side of the gorge. The forest path, lined with horsetails and wood sage, continues for three-quarters of a mile to a gate. In the trees on either side goldcrests whisper. Beyond the gate the forest continues on one side and pastures slope away on the other. Ahead are glorious views of the Sound. Overhead a pair of buzzards circle, enjoying the rising air currents. Beyond the next gate lies the burial ground and the second car.

*Wild strawberry*

*4¹/₂ miles*
*3 hours*

# 20. Torrylin Cairn, Kilmory

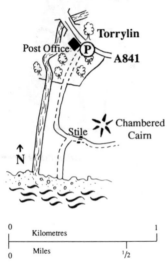

Torrylin

Post Office

A841

Stile

Chambered
Cairn

N

| 0 | | | 1 |
|---|---|---|---|
| Kilometres | | | |

| 0 | | | |
|---|---|---|---|
| Miles | | ¹/₂ | |

**O.S. reference 957215**

Park close to the Kilmory store, post office and tearoom. The ancient monument is clearly signposted. Walk along the path through a lush deciduous wood of ash and sycamore, with rhododendrons and ferns forming a dense undergrowth. Beneath these grows a carpet of wood sorrel leaves. Deep in the ravine to the right of the path is Kilmory Water, surging dark brown over its bed and foaming white where rocks inhibit its progress.

As the path climbs, blue tits chatter in the beech trees lining the path. Beyond these trees the woodland ceases and there are good views of the sea and pastures where cows chew their cud.

The path is now bordered with hawthorn bushes and in one, a fledgling spotted flycatcher calls shrilly. Its parents dart through the bushes, feeding it assiduously. The verges are full of flowers and here ragwort, pink and white clover, bramble, meadow sweet, thistle, vetch, red campion, cleavers and honeysuckle bloom. Beyond the hawthorn are gorse bushes in which several yellow hammers call. One, a male with bright yellow head and chestnut coloured lower back, sits on a branch and utters its striking call, 'A little bit of bread of no cheese'. On the 'cheese' it opens its pale

*Yellow hammer*

brown beak very wide. Below, Kilmory Water races to loose its energy in the sea.

To the left of the path, wooden steps give access to the prehistoric chambered cairn, which was built probably between 3000 B.C. and 2500 B.C. It originally consisted of a passage divided into four compartments (some of the stones of which can still be seen), roofed with stone slabs. The whole was buried under a long earth mound. When excavated about eighty years ago the remains of at least six adults, a child and an infant were found. The site is walled on the sea side and has a wire fence around the remainder. Cows, curious of visitors, peer over the wire.

The site is now almost covered with flowering grasses among which grow clover, ragwort, harebells, yarrow, hawkbit and hogweed. Ring doves, probably having nested near King's Cave, Drumadoon, fly overhead, showing the white patch on their necks and transverse white bars on their wings.

This is a short but delightful walk in rain or shine.

*1 mile*
*¹/₂ hour*

*Chambered cairn*

67

# 21. Kilmory Church, Aucheleffan, Auchareoch, Kilmory Church

O.S. reference 963218

Travelling east, take the first turning on the left after the Lagg Hotel and follow the road as it bears to the right. Park beyond Kilmory Church in a large grassy space edged with ash and hazel. Walk back along the road and take the cart track that goes to the right. Meadow sweet, foxgloves, salad burnet and hogweed flower in profusion.

*Kilmory Church*

The track crosses the Kilmory Burn and then begins to climb steeply. Mistle thrushes 'churr' in the trees above and a buzzard is disturbed from its snooze on a fencing post. Harebells, ragwort, scabious and campion colour the verges, and honeysuckle flowers abundantly.

At the next house keep straight on, following the grassy path, which is hedged with hawthorn and beech, until the gated entrance to the forest is reached.

The path continues for nearly two miles along a narrow ride through the forest. In places it is wet, with juncus, marsh stitchwort, marsh thistle, bog asphodel, water mint and butterwort flourishing. But these small boggy areas can be circumvented by tracking through the banks of heather on either side of the path.

The forest is made up of various conifer species, the trees marching on and on in all directions. Chaffinches call from the trees that edge the ride and dozens of young coal tits inspect the cones and needles for insects. A wren scolds as it is disturbed. Swallows flash down the ride enjoying the midges and flies that plague the walker. Overhead a raven glides leisurely.

An old drystone wall borders the path just before it begins to slope downhill towards Aucheleffan. Forget-me-nots grow in

*Coal tit*

boggy pools, together with the tall marsh lousewort and yellow pimpernel.

And then this trek through the trees ends at a small clearing around the farm of Aucheleffan. Sheep, geese and calves graze and dogs rush out to meet the visitors.

Cross the small burn by a step - with care if it is swollen by the previous night's rain - and follow the path through the farm, where many foxgloves grow with two pure white among the pink.

A wide sandstone track sweeps through the forest. Trees lie back from either side and extra light has increased the variety of flowering plants. Here are orchis, pink and white, flowering together with angelica, heath, heather, tormentil, yellow rattle, wild valerian, and the ubiquitous foxgloves. Siskin fly across the ride and more coal tits flit restlessly from branch to branch.

Once the Allt an t-Sluice Burn is crossed look for a right turn leading downhill to Auchareoch. Pass through two gates at the farm and then continue along the dirt track. In the fields around the farm are horses and cattle, and the verges along the track are filled with a mosaic of yellow and purple flowers.

The serried ranks of conifers crowd in on either side as the path continues for another mile until a gate gives access to the open moorland.

Walk along the track for another mile. Across to the right lies the path hidden in the forest, high up on the ridge, taken much earlier. Kilmory Church can be seen across the intervening moor and fields on the right.

Take the cart track that goes off to the right. As it swings away to a house continue along a narrow path between tall hedgerows. Again a myriad of wild flowers delights the eye. Join a cart track and, when this branches, bear right to return to the church and the car.

*6 miles*
*3$^1$/$_2$ hours*

*Aucheleffan*

# 22. Black Cave, Bennan Head

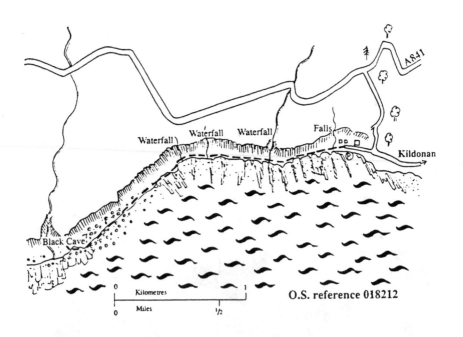

O.S. reference 018212

Drive along the cart track to the provision store at the west end of Kildonan and park facing out to sea opposite the store. Walk on past two cottages and then along a path that sometimes follows the shore and at others goes over a grassy raised beach. Just beyond the cottages a waterfall tumbles, noisily and elegantly, over a cliff face.

The path is bordered with tansy. To the right of the raised beach are cliffs covered with trees. On a dead branch of one a heron stands, its head sunk between its hunched-up shoulders. Lesser

*A waterfall tumbles noisily and elegantly over a cliff face.*


black-back gulls fly slowly over the waves and hooded crows probe in the grass. Another waterfall is passed.

After a quarter of a mile, the walker reaches a small bay between dykes, where fifty or more common seals bask. Some lie alone on a well-rounded boulder, and a female and her two pups share another. Twenty or thirty females sunbathe together on a dyke running out to sea. They lie so still that at first sight they seem like clay models. Then a tail swings into the air or a pup nudges its parent.

Eiders swim in small family parties and several cormorants hang out their wings to dry. Grey wagtails cavort around the rocks. Just beyond the basking seals a huge waterfall leaps in long white strands of water to cascade over ridges and ledges of rock found towards its base. After its exultant drop, the burn races across the raised beach to the sea.

Continue along the shore past another waterfall falling over red sandstone cliffs. Dune cranesbill, thrift, buttercups, beautiful St. John's wort, red campion, clover, hawkweed, marsh sorrel, cat's ear, silver weed, corn chamomile and self heal carpet the ground. Another waterfall is passed. Along the beach wheatears flit from rock to rock. The path passes over grass and shore for about a mile. Then the way becomes more rocky. Towards the cliffs grow bracken, bramble and gorse, and here are several families of whinchat. The male, with its conspicuous eyestripe, white patches on the wing, rufous chin and light coloured breast, repeats its harsh insistent call swaying from the top of a ragwort plant. Two young willow warblers flutter around a nearby bush.

Then the path ceases and for half a mile or so the walker has to scramble over rocks that are easier to circumvent or climb than they seem. Among the great boulders grow thrift, stonecrop, harebells, ivy, fern, campion, agrimony, wood sage and cranesbill.

The boulders become larger but they are not rough or jagged and there is always an easy way. And then, if the tide is high, your way appears to be barred by the cliff face, with the sea lapping at its base. Climb round on the conveniently stepped black rocks but keep only a few feet above the shallow water rather than climbing higher, over the yellow lichened rocks. Young and old seem to enjoy the scramble.

Then the Black Cave is reached. Its roof is very high and most dramatic. It has an exit at the back with a little path leading up the cliff behind.

*Seals bask*

*Black Cave*

The walk to Black Cave presents a challenge, and reaching it is the reward. On the return the distances do not seem quite so far or the rocks so arduous. As one repasses the seals they start a haunting serenade, which floats eerily on the early evening air. The whinchats scold from their gorse bush as, out to sea, the sun illuminates the columnar cliffs and the lighthouse on Pladda. Ailsa Craig appears above a skirt of mist.

*Ivy*

*4 miles*
*3 hours*

# 23. Loch Garbad, near Kildonan

A long cart track runs from the coast road at Kildonan to a farm named Ballymeanochglen. The main coast road cuts this cart track in two and where this happens it is possible to park on the shore side of the road, leaving the car close into the hedge. If approaching from the direction of Kilmory look for the cart track a quarter of a mile beyond the turn off for Kildonan.

Walk up the long cart track to the farm. In late August smaller plants grow in profusion below hawthorn - ragwort, kidney vetch, knapweed, meadow sweet, red campion, harebells, horse-tails, red bartsia, yarrow, marsh woundwort, foxgloves, rose-bay willow-herb, forget-me-

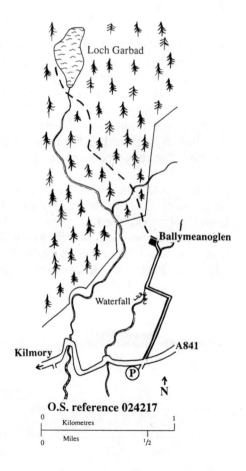

O.S. reference 024217

77

nots, strawberry headed clover, St. John's wort, scabious, eyebright and bell heather. The hawthorn lines both sides of the track and beyond are fields with sheep and cows.

*Hooded crow*

At the second gate keep straight ahead, passing beside a barn. Follow the track as it bears to the left. Pass through another gate out onto the open moorland. Here hooded crows feed by a farm wall made of huge boulders without mortar. Wheatears sit on scattered rocks. The next gate leads into a wide, deeply rutted track through an extensive Forestry Commission plantation. Many of the ruts are full of water and a way has to be found round these, but as soon as the track begins to climb the way becomes easier.

Pause often and look back at Ailsa Craig, the great syenite mound rising out of the sea, and Pladda (Norse for a flat island), both floating on a sea of sparkling glass. The immature conifers that border the ride march away into the distance and host numerous coal tits and goldcrests. Heather and juncus border the edges of the track. In the wetter areas large-headed self heal

*Pladda and Ailsa Craig*

*Loch Garbad*

thrives. Dragonflies, sometimes in tandem, dart above the damp
peat. Blackbirds and robins flit across the ride and the air is full
of the chirping of grasshoppers. Daddy-long-legs, newly emerged,
fill the air.

The path through the forest climbs for three-quarters of a mile
and then comes close to a stream almost choked with parsley and
water dropwort, the latter growing tall and purple stemmed. The
ride swings sharply to the right but the walker should continue
straight ahead to a broken style. Beyond, walk along a little path
for a few yards, and then step across the burn where the
well-trodden track leads. Climb up the sloping bank and ahead
lies Loch Garbad. What a pleasure it is after climbing through the
trees to come to this oval stretch of water surrounded by a steep
bank completely clad in purple heather. On the other side of the
water rises Cnoc na Garbad, a small hill covered with young
conifers and heather. This is the place for the day's picnic.

On the return walk, downhill at last, the sun warms one's face,
and the sea stretches to the horizon, its islands floating like leaves
on a pond. In the far distance Ireland is a faint smudge.

*3¹/₂ miles
2 hours*

# 24. Kildonan Castle

Leave the shore road at the sign for Kildonan. Park on a wide, grassy verge near to the coastguard station and close to Craig End. Note for a later excursion that across the road from this verge a path drops down the cliff to a picnic area and then runs on to the sandy shore below.

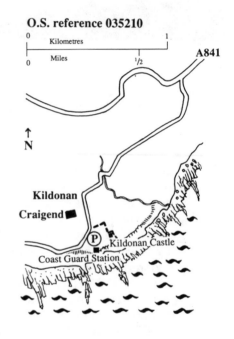

O.S. reference 035210

Walk eastwards from the wide verge for 100 yards. Where the road swings to the left, follow a cart track that leads straight on through a farm gate that lies open.

Young meadow pipits flock, swallows twitter on the wires and wheel overhead, and young chaffinches flit from bush to bush. All kinds of summer flowers border the cart track. Then the medieval keep is seen, tall but still proud, towards the shore.

Follow the track as it passes behind the first cottage on the right and then keep walking straight ahead when the tarmac ceases. Kildonan Castle lies to the left. Its stones are covered with lichen, ivy and sea campion. Around it are hawthorn bushes where a pair

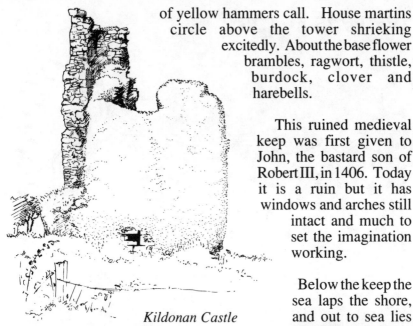

of yellow hammers call. House martins circle above the tower shrieking excitedly. About the base flower brambles, ragwort, thistle, burdock, clover and harebells.

This ruined medieval keep was first given to John, the bastard son of Robert III, in 1406. Today it is a ruin but it has windows and arches still intact and much to set the imagination working.

Below the keep the sea laps the shore, and out to sea lies Pladda with its lighthouse, pristine white in the sunshine. Further out, and to the right of Pladda, is the great rock Ailsa Craig. Clouds flirt with its peak.

*Kildonan Castle*

Inland a huge waterfall tumbles down the hillside and the noise of its falling water can be heard at the keep.

$^1/_2$ *mile*
*10 minutes*

*Lighthouse on Pladda*

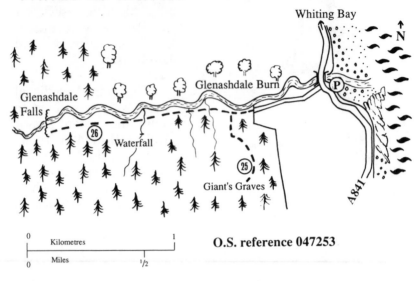

O.S. reference 047253

# 25. Giant's Graves, Whiting Bay

The Giant's Graves lie in a sun-filled clearing sheltered from the prevailing winds by dense conifers.   These chambered tombs, now roofless and lying in ruins were built between 3500 and 2200 B.C.   Each tomb has two large upright stones at one end which were probably part of the entrance.   How were they levered into position and embedded in the ground so securely that 4,000 years later they are still standing?

To visit this interesting site drive to the south end of Whiting Bay and park in a lay-by beside the 'bus shelter on the south side of Glenashdale Burn. Cross the road to where a signpost points the way to the Graves. Follow a cart track that continues to a stile giving access into a Forestry Commission planting. The track is bordered by red campion, shirt buttons, meadow sweet, ragwort, knapweed, pink clover, meadow vetchling, flags, common comfrey, ivy, wild fuchsia, ferns, horsetails, purple loosestrife and rose-bay willow-herb and shaded by sycamore, ash, hawthorn, beech, willow and alder.

*Giant's Graves*

Climb the stile and walk on to a division in the path. Take the left fork signposted to the Graves. After several rain-storms the path is very wet but the steeper slopes have been stepped with attractive log buttresses making ascent easier. A wren scolds from a nearby thicket and wild raspberries grow by the path. Honeysuckle laden with blossom perfumes the air.

*Wren*

Further on conifers line one side of the path and deciduous trees the other. Wood sorrel leaves cover the gound beneath. The dappled sunshine makes this a pleasing walk.

Where the path continues beneath beech trees, mountain fern, hard fern and buttercups thrive along the edges. Soon the beech are replaced by a dense stand of conifers, devoid of ground cover and bird song. Only the wind tangling the tree-tops disturbs the profound silence. A deep carpet of brown needles covers the gound below the trees. At the top of the steepest stretch of the path the larches are widely scattered and sunshine comes streaming through, encouraging a rich growth of brambles, ferns, shirt buttons and red campion.

Follow the rising path as it swings to the right. Use the convenient larch roots as steps. Then the walker reaches a signpost directing him to the left along a level area of the hillside. Conifers stretch in all directions but in small sunny clearings blue tits flit across the opportunist vegetation and coal tits and goldcrests chatter continuously as they work through the needles of the trees edging this patch of light.

Beyond one larger clearing the path, deeply littered with needles that deaden one's footsteps, opens out into a wide ride arched overhead by branches. From these a solitary robin 'tics'. Through the occasional, but rare, breaks in the trees the land can be seen sloping steeply downhill to Whiting Bay, and there are tantalising views of the sea, sandy bays and Holy Island. High overhead the branches of the spruce are covered with raindrops after a short shower and each droplet catches the sunlight and sparkles.

Then the path emerges into the sunlight once more and into the clearing where bracken, rowan and flowering grasses fill the spaces between the graves and other interesting stones.

*1¹/₂ miles*
*1 hour*

# 26. Whiting Bay, south side of Glenashdale Burn, Glenashdale Falls, Whiting Bay

Park the car and walk to the place in the Forestry Commission's woodland where the path divides (see the previous route to the Giant's Caves, Walk 25). Continue straight on where for a quarter of a mile the path is reinforced and passes close to the fast flowing, peat-stained Glenashdale. Its banks are lined with alders and these continue when the reinforcement ends. The path continues all the way to a railed area overlooking the dramatic falls and, though often muddy, is easy to follow. The walker should look for small diversions, convenient boulders and tree roots to help him over the wettest patches.

*Honeysuckle*

Sycamore, birch, ash, beech, and alder fill the glen. Honeysuckle, enchanter's nightshade, red campion, self heal, climbing corydalis, shirt buttons and bell heather flower along the verges of the path. The seed heads of bluebells remind the walker of the beauty of the woods in spring. Many delicate species of fern flourish under the trees and liverworts line damp areas under the tree roots.

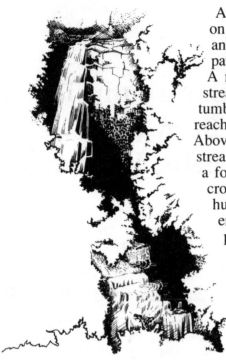

A small side stream is crossed on bright red sandstone slabs and then after half a mile the path climbs the side of the gorge. A racing white-topped feeder stream crosses the path ahead, tumbling down steep slopes to reach the Glenashdale far below. Above the path this impetuous stream leaps down a precipice in a foaming waterfall. A shrew crosses in front of the walker, hungry for insects after an enforced fast during the last prolonged shower. Blue tits chuckle in nearby birches and robins, wrens and chaffinches abound.

*Glenashdale Falls*

The path widens and rises sharply where it passes through a plantation of conifers and finally leads to the viewing platform. Ahead and below lie the magnificent falls. Two great, splendid jets plummet down the precipitous drop into the ravine far below. Impeding ridges and ledges send spray far into the air and the canyon is filled to overflowing with the noise of falling water.

*2¹/₂ miles*
*2 hours*

86

# 27. Whiting Bay, north side of Glenashdale Burn, Glenashdale Falls, Whiting Bay

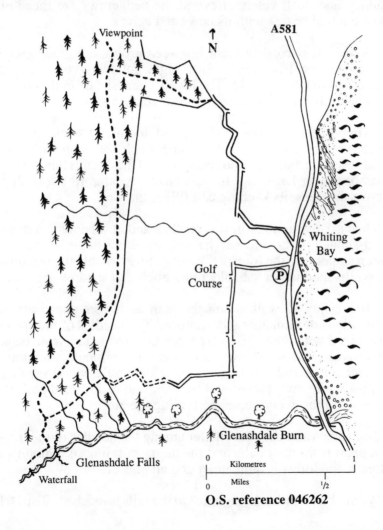

Viewpoint

N

A581

Whiting
Bay

Golf
Course

P

Glenashdale Burn

Glenashdale Falls

Waterfall

| 0 | Kilometres | | 1 |
|---|---|---|---|

| 0 | Miles | 1/2 | |
|---|---|---|---|

**O.S. reference 046262**

Leave the car in the small car park opposite the garage and pier craft centre at Whiting Bay. Walk up the road beyond and above the car park. The road ascends steeply for more than half a mile and then ceases to be metalled as it passes through the buildings and greenhouses of Arran Nurseries.

Turn left at the road that skirts the golf course, which is bordered with brightly coloured fuchsias, honeysuckle, pink campion, kidney and bush vetch. Beyond the hedgerows are meadows where a bull grazes with its cows and calves.

At the cross-roads a giant hogweed grows and greenfinches twitter in the tree tops. Turn right following the signpost directions to Glenashdale. The lovely Glenashdale Falls are seen and heard for the first time from this road.

After half a mile the road is gated and a cart track stretches ahead. Forget-me-nots, orchis, marsh stitchwort, water mint, self heal, angelica, burdock and spearwort fill the ditch. Honeysuckle clambers over hazel and fuchsia alike. A buzzard circles high above the trees, its keening call filling the air.

Then a gate into the forest is reached and, just beyond, a racing peat-stained stream crosses the path and drops impetuously over steep slopes into the forest. Stepping stones enable the walker to cross dryshod under ash, alder and birch that shadow the water.

It is a joy to walk along the path as it continues into the plantations of immature sitka spruce. The needles of the spruce are tinged with blue. The verges are covered with purple banks of cross-leaved heath and large mats of tormentil, making a perfect colour foil. Among these, yellow rattle, wood sage and yellow wort grow. Honeysuckle, white and yellow, and pink and cream, climbs everywhere, perfuming the air.

Goldcrests and coal tits chatter among the needles of the trees, but apart from their calls and the merry gurgling of a mountain stream, the forest is quite quiet and all one's own.

Within half a mile, the signpost to the falls is reached. Turn left

through a compartment of larches and along a recently reinforced path which leads to the top of the huge cataract, where the deeply-stained water surges strongly between confining banks. Walk upstream for twenty yards or so. Here, amid splendid trees and banks of heather, the river descends in a charming, secluded fall.

Return to the top of the main fall and then make a short detour along the edge of the gorge to see the Glenashdale Burn make is two spectacular drops, one of forty feet and the other of 100 feet. From a railed area a very good view of these majestic falls is obtained. A track leads to the bottom, but descent this way is most unsafe and is not advised.

*Secluded fall*

After leaving the falls, rejoin the original track and walk on through the forest. At a T-junction of paths, turn right following a sign pointing towards Lamlash. Look for sneezewort and strawberry-headed clover growing among beds of tormentil and heath. Cat's valerian grows here too.

This track runs parallel with the one taken on entering the forest but is higher up the hillside. The first stream crossed by stepping stones is now recrossed, and once more is seen tumbling exuberantly down steep slopes among the forest trees. A ringlet dragonfly

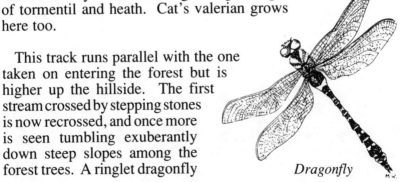

*Dragonfly*

flits back and forth in a clearing, enjoying the warm, humid air of a summer's afternoon.

The forest is alive with tiny noises. A leveret crosses the path ahead and some time later a large hare runs along the track before slipping into the undergrowth. A mile further, a signpost indicates Whiting Bay to the right, but continue ahead for a hundred yards to a picnic table on a grass verge in a clearing. The magnificent view from here should not be missed. Below, beyond the forest slopes, lies Whiting Bay with Holy Island and its lighthouse across the narrow strip of water. Out in the Sound lies Little Cumbrae. To the left are the stark granite peaks on the north of the island silhouetted against a dark blue sky.

Return to the route to Whiting Bay and descend through the forest for a half-mile enjoying the views ahead. At the end of the path turn right and follow a cart track that leads downhill towards the village. Hooded crows feed in the fields that border the track and wild hops and figwort grow in the hedgerows.

Turn right at the next road junction and very soon the car is reached.

*4 miles*
*3¹/₂ hours*

# 28. Kingscross Iron Age Fort near Whiting Bay

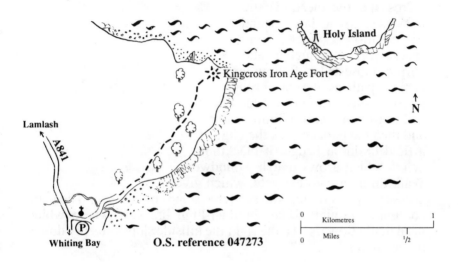

Holy Island

Kingscross Iron Age Fort

Lamlash

A841

N

Whiting Bay          O.S. reference 047273

0       Kilometres       1

0       Miles       ¹/₂

Turn left at the bottom of the hill on the road from Lamlash just as Whiting Bay comes into view and where the signpost for Kingscross Point is clearly visible. Park opposite Whiting Bay Church of Scotland. Follow the road as it bears left (the right fork leads down to the beach).

Continue along a cart track where the road ends. On either side are bracken, gorse, bramble, beautiful St. John's wort and sycamores. Cross the bridge over the burn and follow the cart track as it comes close to the shore. Here in the verge red campion, meadow vetchling and knapweed flower. Out to sea gannets fly and dive and on the shingle beach herring gulls call raucously.

At the end of the cart track climb a small stile on the left into a wet meadow. Follow the track made by other walkers who have found the drier areas. Water mint grows here giving off a pungent odour when crushed by walking boots. The path soon becomes drier and from here there are good views and marvellous sounds of the sea.

Cross the stile ahead. To the left there is a large stand of meadow sweet, some sneezewort and huge headed purple loosestrife. Follow the narrow path as it runs through hazels loaded with nuts. Blue tits and chaffinches call. Climb a slope and then the path crosses the edge of a field beside a hedge of blackthorn, below which grows marsh woundwort. Walk through the next gate, which gives access to open ground with scattered stands of bracken. The path continues through some shoulder-high bracken, where white dead nettle flowers. To the right the hillside slopes steeply down to the shore.

*Hazel*

Then the view opens out and ahead is Holy Island, with its columnar cliffs and the lighthouse snug at its southern tip. Walk along the wide grassy path between more bracken, rose-bay willow-herb, harebells and hawkweed. Ahead are spectacular views of Goatfell and its outliers. Keeping the lighthouse in view walk towards it, through a gap in the gorse. This leads to the Iron Age fort, now just a mound with a small rampart round it. Sit here and, while enjoying the sun, think what a vantage point these ancient folk chose to guard this lovely part of Arran. The sight and sounds of the sheltered Lamlash Bay where, below on the rocks, sandpipers call plaintively and continuously, persuade the walker to linger awhile.

*Iron Age fort*

Why Kingscross Point? Because it was from here that Robert the Bruce made a journey to Turnberry on the mainland. Walk down to the point where the sea laps gently at the rocks and where large stands of sea aster grow.

*2 miles*
*1 hour*

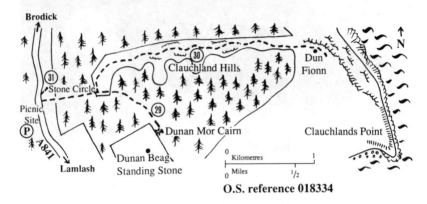

O.S. reference 018334

# 29. Dunan Mor Cairn and Dunan Beag Standing Stone, near Lamlash

When the brow of the hill on the road from Brodick to Lamlash is reached, look for a wide, sandy entrance to a picnic site on the right hand side. Here in a sunny clearing, surrounded by birch, hawthorn and larch, ample parking and several picnic tables have been provided. Robins and chaffinches looking for food fearlessly approach visitors.

Cross the road and continue walking straight ahead over a hillock covered with heather. To the left is a glorious view of the northern mountains, with every line clearly delineated in the bright sunshine. Beyond the hillock join the path leading into a forest ride bordered by bracken and shaded by conifers. Coal tits, blue tits and goldcrests call quietly, hidden among the dense

*House martins*

needles of the trees.
A dragonfly darts along
the ride, and foxgloves
bloom among the bracken, with
tormentil thriving below. At the start
the path is very wet but its condition soon
improves and it is a delight to walk on. A signpost points to the
right, directing the walker to the cairn, and from here the standing
stone is seen, three-quarters of a mile ahead in a green meadow,
with Holy Island and the sea beyond. Follow the narrow path for
half a mile through a wide swathe of very tall bracken with fronds
which in late August are tinged with brown. Overhead house
martins wheel through the air, feasting on
the flies and other insects enjoying the
heat of a summer's day. Meadow pipits
call plaintively from the top of bracken
fronds.

Beyond the bracken that borders the
path are rows of conifers. A small stream
issues from among the trees and threads
its way through the bracken and across
the path. In the moist ground on either
side of the stream thrive St. John's
wort, self heal, meadow sweet,
scabious, horsetails, spearwort,
hardheads, yellow pimpernel, juncus,
marsh thistle and meadow vetchling.
Climbing corydalis, living
parasitically on the roots of the
bracken, grows in great profusion.

*Meadow sweet*

95

A sign points to the Dunan Mor Cairn, which lies to the right of the path. In this Bronze Age burial mound a jet necklace has been found. Now only two stones stand upright and two lie lengthwise on either side. Just behind the cairn is a mound of earth covered with heathers, bilberry, wood sage, tiny rowans and a mass of flowering grasses. From it the walker can see the boats moored in Lamlash Bay and the Dunan Beag Standing Stone, seen earlier on the walk. A signpost directs the walker to the stone but in August it is very difficult to approach because of the tall bracken, dense heather and brambles.

*1½ miles*
*½ hour*

M.W.

*Dunan Mor Cairn*

# 30. Dun Fionn, between Corrygills Point and Clauchlands Point

Park, and walk to the signpost at the end of the forest ride, as for Walk 29. To reach Dun Fionn, an Iron Age fort, turn left at the signpost and follow a good path along the edge of some conifers. Within fifty yards the path swings away from the trees and climbs through dense bracken for a quarter of a mile. Once through the bracken, the path continues for more than a mile along a ridge through glorious, extensive areas of heather, pink and white intermingling with purple. This bonny ridge on the Clauchland Hills delights a multitude of bees and the walker, too. Brodick Bay lies to the north of the ridge and Lamlash Bay to the south. Mature wheatears in fine plumage sit atop a rock or heather stem.

As the path climbs, the sea of heather continues and its beauty in the clear light of a sunny August day is quite breathtaking. Over to the right, as one progresses along the path, the far side of Holy Island comes into view. Where the path comes close to rows of conifers a merlin flies low over the heather and settles. Then it flies up and moves on, revealing its white breast, white flank and dark tail. Once disturbed it is off, flying swiftly with long, narrow

*Merlin*

97

wings into the nearby trees. Blackbirds and a mistle thrush fly into the same trees as they, too, are disturbed. A young, speckled robin, unperturbed, sits fearlessly on a spruce twig and a wren scolds from close by. Rock doves fly overhead.

No traffic sounds, machinery noise or human talk intrude on the peace of this tranquil upland and only the gentle hum of insects breaks the silence of this heathery paradise. After nearly two miles from the start of the walk, the path drops down steeply through bracken to a stile. Beyond the stile climb the steep grassy path ahead that leads to Dun Fionn, the fort on the edge of the headland at the eastern end of the Clauchland Hills. Sheer cliffs defend it on one side and the land slopes sharply downwards on all other sides. The flat top, long and narrow, is covered with springy turf and from here the mountains to the north stand out startlingly clear. Islands float on a glassy sea; the ferry, toy like, comes confidently into harbour. Brodick Castle stands proud against its conifers and sheltering mountain. Dun Fionn provides a wonderful viewing platform for modern day walkers as it did for its defenders long ago.

*4 miles*
*2 hours*

# 31. Stone Circle between Brodick and Lamlash

Leave Brodick in the direction of Lamlash, and park in the only lay-by on the left hand side of the road, just before the brow of the hill.

From here follow the narrow, well-trodden track that crosses a drainage ditch full of summer flowers. It then passes between tall heather, now a riot of colour, to the stone circle.

Four large stones still stand upright with several small stones between. There is a fine view from the circle of Beinn Nuis, Beinn a' Chliabhain and Goatfell.

*A few yards from the road*
*5 minutes*

*View of mountains from the Stone Circle*

# 32.  Glen Rosa, Coire a' Bhradain, rock face of Beinn Nuis,  Glen Rosa

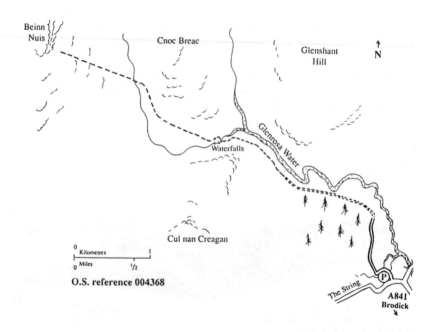

O.S. reference 004368

Park in a small lay-by at the start of the signposted road into Glen Rosa at the Brodick end of The String road.  Walk along the metalled road for a mile and continue when it becomes a rough

cart track. To the left are
conifers and below to the
right winds Glenrosa Water.
To the far right more
conifers stretch away to
Brodick Castle. Ahead lies
the fine glacial valley with
Beinn Nuis, the object of the
walk, veiled in mist. The
valley is very quiet and sheep
graze peacefully.

*White-topped falls*

The cart track becomes a
narrow path, lined with
buttercups and meadow
sweet, and leads to a tall gate
in the high deer fence. The
path continues beyond the
fence, keeping the Rosa Burn
to the right. Where a large
round hillock obstructs the
way take the track to the left
of the hump. Wild thyme,
tormentil, harebells and
lousewort flower among the aromatic bog myrtle.

Now Goatfell lies to the right with the Witch's Step to its left.
Cir Mhor is directly in front with A' Chir to the left. Follow the
path until it reaches the burn that comes down from Coire a'
Bhradain. Along its banks grow butterwort, wood sage, violets
covered with three-pronged capsules, golden rod and round-
leaved sundew. The burn descends through rowan, birch and oak,
in a series of spectacular, white-topped falls racing excitedly to
join the Rosa Burn far below. Cross the foaming stream just
below the weir using the wide granite slabs. Continue climbing
steeply beside the pretty burn through bog asphodel and cotton
grass, indicators of the moisture in the soil. All three heathers
grow here but the dominant vegetation is purple moor grass. This
plant dies at the end of autumn and its dross fills the drainage
ditches thoughout the summer.

The burn makes a right angled turn in its journey across the moor. Continue upwards and bear diagonally to the right, joining a path that leads to the side of the burn, avoiding a very wet triangle of moor. Walk along to the right beside the burn until a suitable crossing place is reached. Check on the steepness of the bank and the presence of suitable boulders to cross the fast flowing water.

After crossing the burn begin ascending the heather-clad slopes below Beinn Nuis, bearing to the right all the time. Among the heather male fern grows resplendent, with both fertile and infertile fronds. Meadow pipits still linger on the high moorland and away on the slopes to the north graze several does.

From here onwards one begins to find aircraft wreckage. Thirty feet below Beinn Nuis' sheer wall of granite, pieces of twisted metal lie jumbled among the rocks and boulders, a sad reminder of the twenty or so lives claimed by this misty peak in three wartime aircrashes. Climb the intervening slope and touch the formidable face of Beinn Nuis, the face that caused the disasters.

*Beinn Nuis*

*6 miles*
*6 hours*

102

# 33. Brodick Standing Stones

Opposite the Arran Craft Centre on the Corrie side of Brodick lies a well sign-posted car park. Park here and walk on towards Brodick, using the grassy verge for safe and easy walking. Within

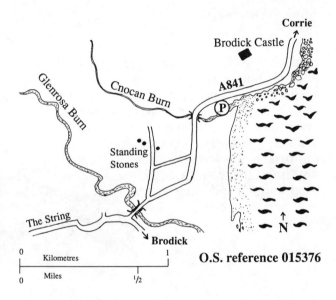

Corrie

Brodick Castle

Glenrosa Burn

Cnocan Burn

A841

P

Standing Stones

The String

Brodick

N

0    Kilometres    1

0    Miles    ¹/₂

**O.S. reference 015376**

under half a mile, on the right hand side of the road, the 'exit' road from the castle joins the main road. Walk along this exit road, for a quarter of a mile, to the end of the long beech hedge that borders it on both sides. Beyond the hedge, walk on up a short rise in the road and look back for the best view of the Standing Stones. Two stand to the right of the road and one to the left. They stand grandly, surrounded by pastures where sheep graze. They can be seen again through convenient gaps in the hedge on the return walk along the drive.

For the writer, the most exciting moment of the walk occurred after her return to the car park. A few yards towards Corrie, the

*Brodick Standing Stones*

road comes close to the shore. Here the protective wall has drainage holes spaced regularly along its base. One of these gave shelter to an unexpected visitor, a nightjar that crouched, exquisitely camouflaged, against dead grass and warm coloured stonework. Walkers, joggers, cyclists and motorists passed by not noticing its rounded head, long tail, sparkling eyes and short beak.

*Nightjar*

$1^1/_2$ *miles*
$^1/_2$ *hour*

# 34. Brodick Country Park and the Seven Bridges Trail

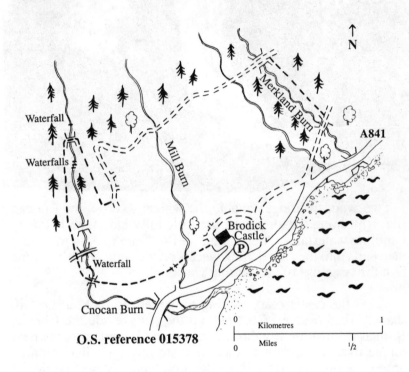

Waterfall

Waterfalls

Mill Burn

Merkland Burn

A841

Waterfall

Brodick Castle

P

Cnocan Burn

0     Kilometres     1

0     Miles     1/2

N

**O.S. reference 015378**

Leave the car in the public car park by the castle. The trail commences close to the front of the castle, beneath some fine beeches. Follow the red way-mark signs. A small burn, Mill Burn, races beneath the track. Iron gates give access to a wild and most pleasurable walk. Enchanter's nightshade, figwort and woundwort bloom along the edges of the path, and young blue tits perkily perform acrobatic feats among the pine needles.

Two wooden bridges enable the walker to cross the Cnocan Burn (meaning the stream of the little hill) and view its lovely tumbling waterfalls. A grey wagtail flits from rock to rock, and then darts into the air catching insects on the wing. Hart's tongue fern thrives close to the surging water.

Cross the castle road, sparing a moment to look at the tall, shapely road bridge. Continue up the path beside the Cnocan Burn as it flows swiftly through its gorge. Do not cross the next bridge over the stream as the red route indicates, but continue uphill, passing through a rhododendron tunnel beside a series of delightful falls to the Duchess's Pool. This is a deep, cold, double pool, constantly kept moving by a tiny fall above it. Trees surround the water, many of them blanketed with moss and supporting polypody fern. In a clearing close by angelica and cow parsley grow.

Cross the bridge constructed in August 1984 by the 74 Engineer Regiment. From here there is a splendid view of a raging waterfall. At the end of this delightful diversion turn left. Coal tits abound in the trees; in the nearby rhododendrons, robins scold, and overhead pigeons fly.

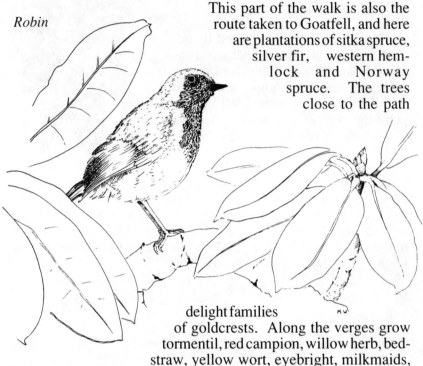

*Robin*

This part of the walk is also the route taken to Goatfell, and here are plantations of sitka spruce, silver fir, western hemlock and Norway spruce. The trees close to the path

delight families of goldcrests. Along the verges grow tormentil, red campion, willow herb, bedstraw, yellow wort, eyebright, milkmaids, self heal, wood sage, yellow rattle and forget-me-nots. Dragonflies dart across the path in the warm, humid air.

The Mill Burn is crossed once more as it noisily makes its way downhill, deep beneath the forest vegetation. Between the trees, to the right, Brodick Bay can be seen, with the ferry boat anchored at the pier.

A shallow burn that can be forded easily is crossed next and in a hundred yards or so the Merkland Burn is spanned by a fine new wooden bridge. Just beyond, follow an arrow directing the walker through a tunnel of dense rhododendrons on the right. This path leads to a Lovers Walk that keeps close to, but well above, the dancing, tumbling Merkland. The burn below is in many places white and in others streaked with brown as it leaps down its long rocky ladder.

This lovely burn is crossed by another bridge and then the path descends towards the shore and Merkland Wood. It passes between deciduous trees and a dense stand of firs, with pastures full of sheep beyond the wall of the wood. And then the castle road is reached. Follow it to the car park.

*Norway*
*spruce*

An exellent way to finish such a splendid day is to visit the castle itself and walk through what has been described by the daughter of the Duchess of Montrose, the last owner of the castle, as 'the most homely home to be shown to the public'.    Walk 36 gives a brief guide to the treasures of Brodick Castle.

*4 miles*
*2¹/₂ hours*

# 35. A Guided Walk through the Gardens of Brodick Castle

These walks, led by the Head Gardener of Brodick Castle, take place on Tuesday afternoons (26th May to 31st August) from 2.30 p.m. to 4.00 p.m.  The Head Gardener has  devoted much of his working life to maintaining and improving these lovely gardens and creating delightful corners, borders, areas and glades. As he talks about the plants, shrubs and trees he draws on his considerable knowledge and reveals his great love for them.

Brodick
Castle

The gardens are renowned for their  immense varieties of rhododendrons. Some species flower in January, others in February and in March, but to see them at their best visit in June.

The eighteenth century walled garden has a wonderful collection of herbaceous plants, riotously coloured and with a multitude of flower heads. The gardens and extensive lawns of springy,  weed-free turf slope away from the castle and there is a summer house with a straw hat roof.

Beyond the walled garden look for the small ponds surrounded by shrubs and trees.  Sit on the bench seats in shady grassy glades

for quiet contemplation. Walk along the narrow paths that wind among small copses and under tall trees many of which have come from distant parts of the globe and enjoy the views of the sparkling waters of Brodick Bay.

One path leads to the Bavarian summer house built in 1845. Its ceiling and the top half of its circular walls are decorated with pine cones set in intricate, formal designs.

In 1958, a year after the death of the Duchess of Montrose (last owner of the castle), Brodick was accepted by the Inland Revenue and the Treasury in lieu of death duties and placed in the care of the National Trust for Scotland. The public were given access to the gardens, and many small paths were added. Today five gardeners look after these lovely grounds.

Visitors who do not wish to join the guided tour may wander through the gardens at will.

*1¹/₂ hours*

# 36. A Walk through Brodick Castle

As the ferry approaches the pier everyone looks with delighted surprise at the lovely bay of Brodick, and at the fine mountains cradling a red sandstone castle, set among plantations of conifers and deciduous trees.

Brodick Castle is open between 1.00 p.m. and 5.00 p.m.

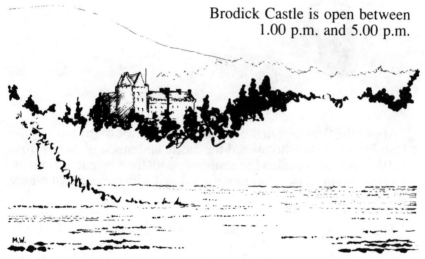

*Brodick Castle*

from Easter until September.  More than 50,000 visitors a year wander through the gardens and the apartments, testimony to the charm and homeliness of the castle.  There is an entrance fee to the gardens and a separate fee for viewing the castle.

*The Entrance Hall*

Above the fireplace in the entrance hall is the coat of arms of the Hamilton family who owned the castle and much of Arran from 1503. The hall and curving staircase, with their bright red carpet, were added in 1844. The staircase is lined with the heads of ninety stags.

The next three rooms were the apartments used by the Duchess of Montrose, the last member of the Hamilton family to live at the castle. She ensured that the castle was well endowed when she gave it into the care of the National Trust for Scotland, in lieu of death duties. The duchess's dressing room, bedroom and boudoir (or sitting room) are visited first. Look for the collection of beautiful fans, the Heppelwhite four-poster bed and its attendant bed table, the marquetry bureau and the sketches by Gainsborough.

112

The long gallery, which is next on the tour, once gave access to the state rooms. The visitor can see the row of footmen's chairs, straight-backed to keep them awake. Look for the beautiful statuettes, some fashioned in silver, ivory or fruitwood, and a set of Sevres porcelain, contained in a glass-fronted showcase.

The drawing room, also erected in 1844, is a gracious room with a magnificent ceiling, an eye-catching conversation (or love) seat and striking soup tureens.

The libary is situated in the part of the castle built at the time of Oliver Cromwell. The book-lined shelves and the ceiling are all in keeping with the severity of the room.

*Soup tureen*

Beyond is the dining room, built in the sixteenth century, where the great table is set for a meal. Admire the splendid ceiling and the delightful wood panelling in this magnificent room.

Downstairs the kitchen and scullery are full of the utensils and domestic equipment used in the last century. The black grates, the heavy pots and pans and the flagged floor remind us of the hard life of those working below stairs.

The last area to be visited is more than 600 years old and includes the vaulted passageway and narrow twisting staircase to Bruce's Room, the part of the castle most evocative of Scottish history.

*2 hours*

# 37. Corrie, Goatfell via Stacach Route, Brodick Castle

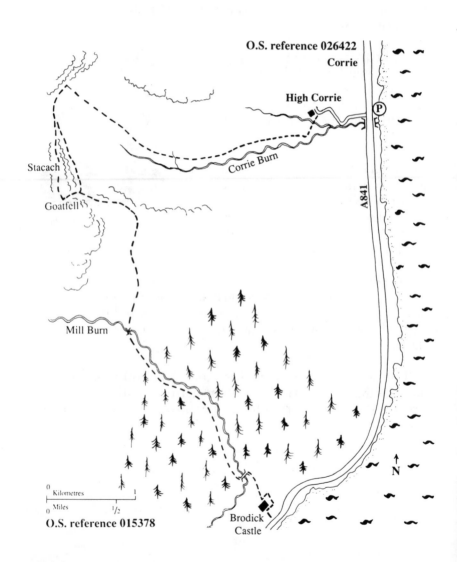

O.S. reference 026422

Corrie

High Corrie

P

Corrie Burn

A841

Stacach

Goatfell

Mill Burn

0 Kilometres 1

0 Miles ¹/₂

O.S. reference 015378

N

Brodick Castle

The walk to Goatfell from Corrie is well signposted and there is ample parking, either on the shore opposite the sign, or in a lay-by further towards the village itself.

From the shore road walk up the cart track that leads to High Corrie. Just before the first house on the left turn left, passing through a signposted gate onto a wide track. Where a first view of a spectacular cascade on the Corrie Burn comes into sight, leave the track, taking the footpath that leads to the right. This climbs steeply up the hillside with the burn on the left and a deer fence to the right.

The path climbs through heather and bracken and after a night's rain can be quite wet. Bog asphodel, milkwort, tormentil and bog myrtle, now with tiny yellow catkins, grow among the bracken. Wheatears and meadow pipits flit in front of the walker.

After three-quarters of a mile a kissing gate in the deer fence leads to a rough steep climb. To the left the Corrie Burn races for many feet over a rock slide before cascading through silver birches full of blue tits. A grey wagtail sits on a boulder, mid-stream, and then darts acrobatically upwards to catch an insect.

The steep climb continues for nearly half a mile and the Corrie Burn delights the eye with its foaming wilfulness. Each drop-let of spray, tossed wantonly into the air, sparkles in the bright sun. Dark pigmented meadow brown butterflies visit the heather and then are attracted to ragwort that thrives along the bank of the burn. Rowan saplings struggle to survive.

*Ragwort and meadow brown butterfly*

Beyond the ridge, the Corrie Burn lies to the left and the ground rises more gently, a relief for one's legs after the steep climb. Hard fern, alpine lady's mantle and bilberry grow here. Away to the left on the lower slopes of North Goatfell are thirty to forty stags, difficult to see at first among the granite boulders. Only when the walker looks carefully does he realise how many there are and how close they are to the path.

After this 'restful' quarter of a mile comes a steep climb to the ridge ahead where sheer granite walls, with a multitude of fractures, rear upwards on either side of the path. Pause here and look over the ridge into Glen Sannox and the steep crags beyond. Notice the dwarf willow that grows like a carpet beneath one's feet.

After enjoying the magnificent view, turn left and decide which route to take to the top of Goatfell. The lower path leads across the mountainside to the last straightforward climb to the top. The upper path is the Stacach route. This involves climbing through a small 'chimney', clambering down some steep rock steps, walking along a flattish area and climbing a 'passage' before starting down more rock steps. All age groups seem to enjoy this exhilarating scramble and clamber. At the end of the Stacach the two paths converge and continue to the summit and its solid cairn.

On a clear day, the views are marvellous in all directions. Close to are the surrounding Arran peaks, with glimpses of Loch Tanna and Loch na Davie. Beyond, to the north, lies Kintyre with sparkling sea on either side of the peninsular. Even further north lie the mountains of Jura and Mull, with the Highland peaks just discernible. To the east Little Cumbrae and the Island of Bute float like toys on blue water. To the south Ailsa Craig rears up out of the sea with Holy Island to its west. The mountains are topped with clouds and far away to the west lies Ireland, a faint darkening on the horizon.

On a summer's day sunbathe and picnic on the summit. It seems impossible that the mountain's name means windy hill. Buttercups flower and meadow pipits flutter about the surrounding boulders.

M.W.

To return leave the summit by continuing onwards and downwards, keeping to the path to the left of the scree. Concentration is required when stepping from boulder to boulder. After half a mile the route levels a little but the path continues downwards and is very wet for much of the way. Juniper hugs the boulders by the path and bell heather, bog asphodel and milkwort flourish. Pause for a break at the small bridge over Mill Burn, the artifical cut that carries the water for Brodick Castle. A dipper, feeding in the racing water, flies up the burn for a quieter place. Below lies Brodick Bay. Refreshed, continue beside the cut which now passes through rows of conifers until a small reservoir is reached.

The track continues to Brodick Castle where, hopefully, a bus awaits, to reunite you with your car at Corrie.

*8 miles*
*6 hours*

# 38. Glen Sannox

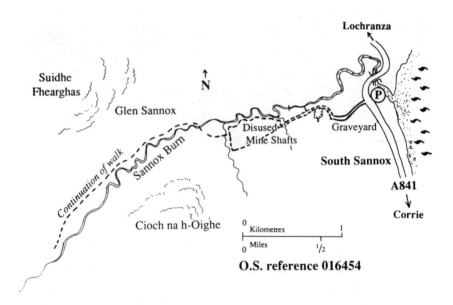

Suidhe Fhearghas

Glen Sannox

N

Lochranza

P

Sannox Burn

Continuation of walk

Disused Mine Shafts

Graveyard

South Sannox

A841

Corrie

Cioch na h-Oighe

0 Kilometres 1

0 Miles ½

**O.S. reference 016454**

Park in open space opposite the signposted cart track to Glen Sannox. Cross the road and pass through the kissing gate and walk along the metalled road. The hedge on the left is of hazel, beech, hawthorn, holly and ash. Deep-pink dog roses grow here too. Sheep graze in a field on the right, and over these dive swallows and house martins after insects that abound wherever stock is present.

Pass the cemetery, with its huge yew, on the left and note the interesting wrought-iron ladder stile that gives access to the burial ground. Young blue tits whisper excitedly among the surrounding bushes and wagtails cavort overhead enjoying youth and the sun.

After this point the cart track begins. It is bordered with bracken, rhododendrons, rowan and birch, and in the grass large eyebright grows erect. Here, in the trees, coal tits 'siss' conspiratorially and pigeons fly overhead.

Climb over a high stile and follow the track, lined with bracken, that continues into the glen. Ahead are Suidhe Fhearghas, Ceum na Caillich, Cir Mhor and Cioch na h-Oighe. One moment their heads are in the cloud, and the next their peaks float ethereally above brilliant white mist that moves and trails below the tops.

*Dog rose*

The turf of the path is starred with tormentil. In the trees to the left young spotted flycatchers make short sallies into the air, then return to their observation posts having caught luckless insects. A wood warbler flies about the branches of young beech. It is larger than the willow warbler, with longer wings and yellow-green plumage.

At the wood end on the right, clamber down the steep slope to the Sannox Burn. It is wide and flows noisily over its boulder-strewn bed. It tumbles, clear and blue, down steep drops under oak, hazel, birch, blackthorn and alder. The sun penetrates the foliage of the latter and catches each droplet that is thrown in the air by the impeding bouiders. Along the burn's banks harebells, tormentil, mountain fern, marsh thistle and tall self heal grow.

Return to the cart track and continue along it. Close by are two

rows of lofty beech. Thyme, heath, milkwort and a very short
eyebright flourish here. The track continues along the edge of a
disused barytes mine and then comes to a tributary that tumbles in
pretty falls on its way to join the main stream. Bog myrtle covers
the ground, with lousewort and common speedwell growing
where it can. Look back to good views of the Clyde.

Walk on along the track past fenced-off mine shafts to where the
burn makes a large curve. Bog asphodel is in flower and a large
tuft grows well in a crevice in a boulder in the middle of the burn.
Meadow pipits soar into the air and descend trilling into the bog
myrtle below. Eventually the path is crossed by a feeder burn.
Follow it down to where, in a pretty hollow, it joins the Sannox.

Returning, follow the path that keeps close to the water's edge.
It soon becomes a wide grassy swathe through the bracken.
Dragonflies hover momentarily before darting across the water,
and deep blue scabious flower close to the path.

Just above the disused mine the burn has a small weir. Below,
a row of large sandstone boulders almost blocks its passage so that

the water is channelled through a very narrow gap. Perhaps this provided a fast flow of water for the derelict water wheel lying close by. At the foot of the fall is a lovely, clear, deep pool with rowan, beech, birch and willow overhanging the water. Just beyond the old water wheel the path joins the cart track used on the outward walk.

If the walker wishes to continue into Glen Sannox there is a good path on the north side of the Sannox Burn. Cross the beck by the ford beyond the feeder stream mentioned earlier, or at any other suitable place beyond the barytes mine. This easy-to-tread path takes the walker deep into the glen and the point from which to commence the climb to the saddle between Glen Sannox and Glen Rosa.

*2¹/₂ miles*
*1 hour*

*Derelict water wheel*

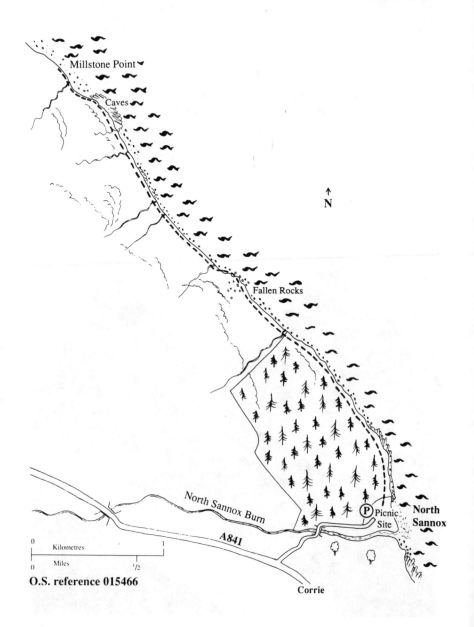

Millstone Point

Caves

N

Fallen Rocks

North Sannox Burn

A841

P Picnic Site

North Sannox

Kilometres
0                                    1

Miles
0                    ¹/₂

**O.S. reference 015466**

Corrie

# 39. Picnic Site at North Sannox to Millstone Point

At the well signposted picnic site at North Sannox the walker will find ample parking and toilet facilities. Walk towards the shore end of the car park and follow a narrow path that bears left though a dense stand of spruce. A short way along the path, a kissing gate gives access to a wide track through Forestry Commission plantings. A narrow screen of birch separates the path from the shore and the deep blue waters of the Sound of Bute. Out to sea gannets fly and dive for food. On the left side of the track crags tower upwards covered with conifers, but the ride itself is deeply edged with ash, birch and rowan.

*Gannets*

The track is bordered by a profusion of flowering plants, and honeysuckle and dog roses are both in bloom. Sheltered from the wind and in the full sun the many flowers attract meadow brown, cabbage white and fritillary butterflies. Grasshoppers chirrup loudly and a giant wood wasp whirrs angrily across the ride. When the screen of birch ends the Sound stretches away to the mainland with herring gulls flying slowly along the shore against the wind.

Further along the track silver fir and western hemlock come down to the edge of the path and in these goldcrests call unconcerned by the 'mee-oo-ing' of a buzzard high on the mountain slope. At the end of the track a picnic table has been set up and beyond this a narrow path leads along the shore with a deer fence on the left. Behind, steep slopes rear upwards covered with bracken and heather. Climb a ladder stile across the fence and follow the little path that leads to the Fallen Rocks. These great red sandstone boulders, studded with pebbles, lie scattered down the hillside and in the sea. A narrow path passes between the huge conglomerate rocks, and the grassy patches among the boulders are just made for picnics and afternoon naps.

Continue along the distinct path, making full use of driftwood placed by earlier walkers over the wetter areas. The high slopes of Corloch occasionally obscure the sun but the path is always a joy to walk along even

*Sedimentary rock layered and angled*

M.W.

124

in the damper areas where the delicate grass of Parnassus flowers together with scabious, thyme, bog asphodel, milkwort and tall sundew. Meadow pipits and wheatears flit ahead and settle on the rocks about the path. Several hoodies fly low across the waves and a peregrine glides over the bracken-covered slopes. Small black tadpoles swim with much tail wriggling in a shallow, sun-warmed pool.

The path comes close to some caves. The largest, filled with fish boxes used as seats and a fishing net, has probably been used for centuries by local fishermen. Above the dark opening the sedimentary rock is fascinatingly layered and angled. Out to sea, a manx shearwater skims and shears the waves showing its black back, white underparts and long black bill with hooked tip. Its wings, slender and pointed, enable it to glide and loiter through the air. A sandpiper calls from rocks about the shore and bobs up and down as it calls.

Another hundred yards and Millstone Point is reached. This is a splendid walk with glorious views across the Sound and easy walking for much of the way.

*5 miles*
*3 hours*

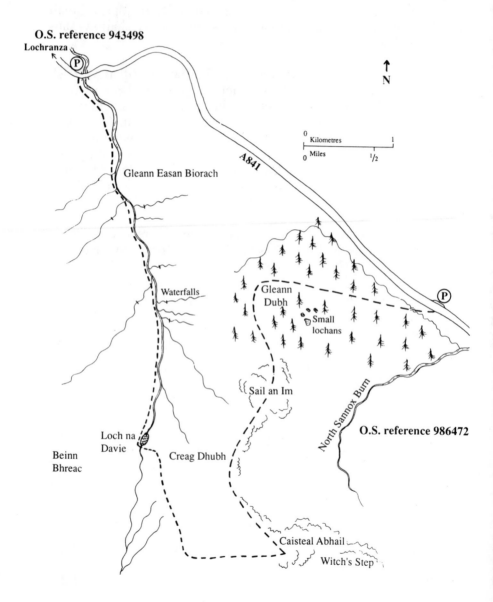

O.S. reference 943498

Lochranza

N

0 Kilometres 1

0 Miles 1/2

A841

Gleann Easan Biorach

Waterfalls

Gleann Dubh

Small lochans

Sail an Im

North Sannox Burn

O.S. reference 986472

Loch na Davie

Beinn Bhreac

Creag Dhubh

Caisteal Abhail

Witch's Step

# 40. The Boguillie, Caisteal Abhail, Loch na Davie, Glenn Easan Biorach

If driving from the direction of Lochranza, park in a signposted lay-by on the left hand side, just before the North Sannox Burn. Cross the road and walk over the rough moorland to a gate in the deer fence. Inside the fence is an extensive planting of tiny spruce. The terrain has been dyked and planted and the going is very rough. There are no paths. Follow the dykes wherever these help and walk to the right in the direction of Gleann Dubh, steadily climbing all the time. If the walker keeps to the far right on ascending (though not as far as the small stream Abhainn Tunna in the Gleann) he will avoid the very wet area and the small lochans on the plateau above.

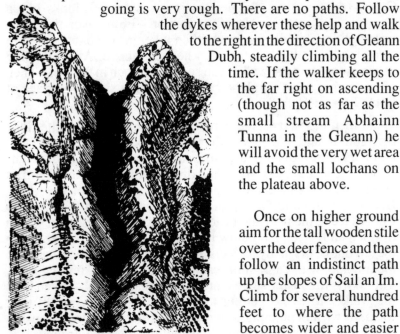

*The Witch's Step*

Once on higher ground aim for the tall wooden stile over the deer fence and then follow an indistinct path up the slopes of Sail an Im. Climb for several hundred feet to where the path becomes wider and easier

*Golden rod*

to follow. Far below lies the rocky desolation that spawns North Sannox Burn and its tributary. Among the rocks a small herd of does finds some vegetation to feed on and one lies asleep. The track goes on and on and always upward. The Witch's Step lies over to the left and Cir Mhor and Goatfell beyond. Pause and look back and around. You seem to have reached the top of the world, with the Firth of Clyde, Loch Fyne, Bute Sound and Kilbrannon Sound sparkling and placid around the skirts of Arran.

The slopes are covered with heather, clubmosses, bilberry, tormentil, bedstraw, alpine lady's mantle, crowberry, golden rod and alpine willow. Directly ahead lies Caisteal Abhail or The Castles, the second highest point on Arran. It looks like a sleeping warrior. From over the slope ahead glides a golden eagle and then it begins to soar and soar in a great spiral until lost in the misty heavens above. After climbing several more feet the walker can see Dubh Loch in the west. Then after another short climb he can see the long shining surface of Loch Tanna (Walk 3).

And then the first Castle is reached. Continue along the ridge between it and the next where the ground is covered with boulders, grains of eroded granite and thin grass. A pair of ravens fly overhead and then wheel and dive, delighting in the thermals and the sun. Walk on a little further to see more of Cir Mhor, Beinn Tarsuiin and the top of Ben Nuis. Between the first two Castles leave the tops and head down the mountainside in search of Loch na Davie. Far below lies the snaking Iorsa Water and to the left one of the many lochans in Glen Iorsa. Keep moving down the hillside, with care, until reaching a good path, running right. This skirts the lower slopes far below Creag Dhubh and enables the walker to avoid getting tangled up in some very difficult rock-strewn and precipitous terrain. Heather and bilberry bushes laden with berries with a glorious bloom cover the ground.

After half a mile along the narrow path Loch na Davie lies to the left. Keep a watchful eye for the little lochan as it is easy to by-pass because it remains hidden below a small hillock. The Iorsa Burn flows out of the south end of the lochan and from the northern end issues the Easan Biorach. Loch na Davie has the distinction of being the only lochan on Arran to have burns leaving it from either end. Cross the south end of the lochan by a little rock weir and then head north along the track that runs for the whole length of Gleann Easan Biorach. From the path, very wet in places, one can enjoy the lovely burn as it descends in many fine waterfalls and cascades through rock gardens and under several service trees. A male merlin hunts here, its orange rump very bright in the afternoon sun. A young linnet sits atop a heather twig and calls quietly, its breast softly suffused with pink.

The path leads through the gorge, beside the waterfall and down to the road below Ballarie, past rowans heavy with berries. Hopefully a kind friend with a car, or the bus, will return you to your car two miles south along the road.

*7 miles*
*7 hours*

*Caisteal Abhail (The Sleeping Warrior)*

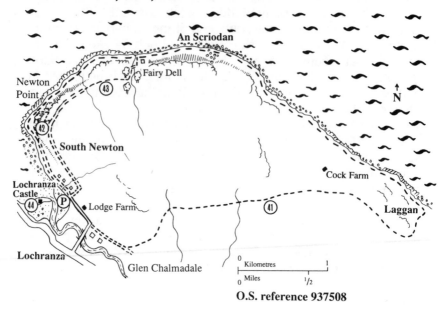

O.S. reference 937508

# 41. South Newton, Laggan, An Scriodan, Newton Point, South Newton

Take the side road opposite the Loch Ranza Field Centre, close to milestone 44. Cross the bridge over the Chalmadale Burn and turn left at the end of the road. Park on a verge by the shore just beyond Lodge Farm and walk back along the road to the signpost indicating the direction to take for Laggan. The way lies straight ahead along a cart track with bracken growing on one side and cottages set among trees on the other. The track, bordered by harebells, foxgloves, tormentil, bell heather and meadow vetchling climbs gently. Where the track drops downhill follow a signposted grassy path that continues climbing. Overhead

130

scream swallows and house martins as they feast on the myriad of insects in the warm summer air. Robins and chaffinches twitter from nearby scrubby hawthorn bushes.

*Wide sunny track*

The wide sunny track through the bracken attracts butterflies, and dragonflies abound. Grasshoppers call from all directions and occasionally one hops onto a boulder by the path. A merlin, flying silently and menacingly, wings low over the heather slopes that have now replaced the bracken. A flock of twites dart indecisively through the warm air, all twittering at once as they go. Cross a small burn, shadowed by birches, willows and ferns, by a wooden bridge beyond which the path continues to climb steadily. Ahead are splendid views of the Sleeping Warrior (Caisteal Abhail) and the surrounding heights. Several female deer can be seen on both sides of the path, but they are high up and safe from the intrusive walker and her dog.

Where the path comes close to a noisy beck, drawing water from the slopes around, low growing birch, rowan and willow thrive. These shrubs, cut down by winter winds, cannot grow above the sheltering banks of the burn. Milkwort, sundew and butterwort abound on both sides of the path. The path crosses a moorland plateau, which is covered with juncus and cotton grass. The area is very marshy but if the walker picks his way carefully he will remain dryshod. As the path climbs to the shoulder, slate litters the way and then, once the ridge is attained, the Sound of Bute lies below with tiny boats appearing becalmed on its glassy surface. Gannets, pristine white, fly and dive far below.

Follow the path as it begins to wend downhill. The quietness of the lovely summer's day is broken only by the croak of a raven and the keening of a buzzard. To the right of the path the steep craggy slopes of Creag Ghlas rear up and on these a peregrine has raised her brood. To the left steep, bracken-clad slopes run down to ruined crofts, including Cock Farm where Harold Macmillan's ancestors lived. Continue along the wide grassy path, edged with white harebells. After a mile another ruined croft lies ahead, and just before this the path swings to the left and drops down and down to the shore beside Laggan Cottage.

Turn left by the cottage and follow the track along a raised beach through the bracken and a multitude of summer flowers. Close to the path the clear blue water of the Sound laps pale-grey sandstone boulders. Where an alder and birch wood lies ahead, take the path that runs just above the shore and below the trees. The going, rough a times but clear, passes over a carpet of skull cap and handfuls of coal can be picked up from the remains of a thin coal seam. Beyond the trees is the site of the old harbour of the Laggan settlement where lived a farming community in the eighteenth century. A small industry flourished here, using the coal to

*Cock Farm*

M.W.

produce salt from sea water for curing fish. On the heights above to the left deer are silhouetted against a clear blue sky and ravens glide.

Continue along the path, which soon passes great blocks of red limestone on the shore. Out to sea a common seal watches the walker and hoodies fly low over the water. Oystercatchers, herring gulls and lesser black-back gulls preen on the rocks. Soon the cliffs of Torr Breac tower so high that the cliff face and the shore lie in dense shade. The trees at the foot of the sheer slopes are alive with willow warblers, wood warblers, blue tits and spotted flycatchers. Another seal surfaces and peers inquisitively.

The walker now comes to a great rock fall. This is not the Fallen Rocks named on the O.S. map through which runs an easy grassy path for walking. This is An Scriodan, where 250 years ago innumerable great boulders of sandstone tumbled from high above. Follow the path through these. The way is not always easy and some scrambling is required. Then walk on along the shore towards the cottage at 'Fairy Dell' the path becoming much wetter as a result of the impermeable nature of the underlying schist. The path is easy to follow, having been well trampled, but it is very wet. Make full use of strategically-placed rocks and driftwood. Past the cottage the walk continues, equally wet, but beyond Newton Point lies the road and soon the end of South Newton shore is reached and the starting point of the walk.

*8 miles*
*6 hours*

133

# 42. South Newton and the hill above

Take the right turn opposite the Loch Ranza Field Centre, west of milestone 44. Cross the bridge over the Chalmadale Burn and continue along the shore road for a quarter of a mile. Park on a grass verge on the left at the head of the bay. Walk on along the shore road to its end and here watch the herring gulls fly into the air each with a mussel in it yellow and red bill. Each gull drops its mussel trophy onto rocks below, picking it up and dropping it again, time after time, until the shell is broken and its contents can be gobbled up.

*Herring gull*

At the road end continue over the grassy, and freqently muddy, area beyond, using a track just below the low cliffs covered with birch and oak. A hundred and fifty yards beneath the trees a path, called by locals the 'secret path', climbs up through hazels and oaks until the bracken-covered and grassy slopes above are attained. Convenient rocks provide useful steps for making the ascent easier. Pass through the bracken beyond the trees and turn right. Enjoy the glorious view of the bay and the amphitheatre of heights. A frigate passes silently up the Sound of Kilbrannon and a small fishing boat bobs about on the white-topped water. Seals rest on projecting rocks just off shore.

A row of straggly hawthorns bearing a good crop of haws lies ahead. Pass through the trees by a convenient gap. Continue on and at the next hedgerow turn left and climb uphill to the 'scenic route', the cart track that gives access to the cottages high above South Newton. Pause here again for a glorious view of the mountains and perhaps a glimpse of a rainbow passing through the clouds and dipping into the sea. Turn right along the road and follow it downhill to the shore. Turn left to where the car is parked.

*Hawthorn*

*1¹/₂ miles*
*1 hour*

# 43.  South Newton, Fairy Dell, Newton Point, South Newton

Park as for Walk 42 and walk on for twenty yards.  Turn right and walk up the cart track that leads from the shore road to the houses along the 'scenic route'.  In late May hawthorns and rowans, both laden with blossom, line the track and in the grassy verge below the trees bluebells, shirt buttons and ramsons flower.  After half a mile the track becomes a path through the cliff-top pastures where milkweed, tormentil, lousewort and butterwort spangle the ground.  The path keeps close to the edge of the cliffs and below the walker a pair of hooded crows plane on the air currents and then return to their nest in the trees on the wooded slopes.  Away to the right over Cnoc nan Sgrath a buzzard sails across the tops as it is harried by a dozen jackdaws and they scatter noisily.  The buzzard flaps once and then, indolently, sails off to its brood on the crags.

Continue along the path to where it drops steeply towards the shore, passing through a small wooded area.  Here beside the stream grow primroses, violets and bluebells.  Cross the plank bridge and walk on down to the shore and Fairy Dell. Bear right at the shore, past a white-washed cottage, to a dyke formed by a ridge of granite lying athwart the beach.  The ridge became

*Buzzard harried  by jackdaws*

*Violets*

exposed when the sand-stone covering was eroded. The dyke acts like a break-water; on the west side of the dyke vegetation cannot take hold, but on the other side, protected from the furies of the sea, many kinds of seaweed grow. Here on the shore a ringed plover calls and elevates its tail into a fan. It trails a wing, first one side and then the other, then it runs up the shore and repeats this puzzling performance. We pause behind a boulder and after a few minutes the parent bird is seen leading two fluffy chicks away in the opposite direction.

Return along the raised beach bordering the shore, picking the driest path among the cow wheat that grows, parasitically, on the roots of previous years' heather. Silver weed, with bright yellow flowers and silvery leaves, trails among the pebbles of the beach. English stonecrop blooms in the crevices between the rocks. Herb robert, tom thumb, thrift, bedstraw and yellow pimpernel thrive in the drier parts and where it is wetter recumbent hawthorns, willows and roses flourish. In the very wet marsh flower flags, milkmaids, kingcups, spearwort, cotton grass and upright sundew and the ditches are full of broad-leaved pondweed.

Off the shore a family of eider float along, three females, one male and several young. The adults leap slightly into the air before they dive headlong into the waves for food. Gannets wing strongly overhead and seals sunbathe on the rocks, which are now well above the retreating tide. Continue along the beach to Newton Point and then join the road that runs along South Newton shore where sandpipers, which breed here every year, scold their young to stop them straying into danger. A cuckoo flies from the trees behind the cottages across Loch Ranza to woods on the opposite side. Walk on along the shore until you regain your car.

*3¹/₂ miles*
*1¹/₂ hours*

# 44. Lochranza Castle

The ruined Lochranza Castle has the sea on three sides and is never more picturesque than when the tide is full and the sun is setting in a ball of fire. Park on a grass verge in the middle of the village. The

*Lochranza Castle*

castle lies on a spit of gravel projecting into the loch. The key is obtained from the post ofice in the village. Look for the address and the times for obtaining the key on a board close to the narrow road leading along the spit.

Of the original castle built in the fourteenth century little remains. The existing structure dates from the sixteenth century, with some of the earlier structures incorporated. In 1897 a square turret collapsed but in recent years the fabric has been maintained. Today the roofless building is an exciting place to visit, with its stairs and steps to the various levels and the slits and other openings in its walls.

*Slits and openings*

*¹/₂ hour*

# Clan Walks

A series of walks described by Mary Welsh, covering some of the most popular holiday areas in the Scottish Highlands and Islands.

Titles published so far include:

1. 44 WALKS ON THE ISLE OF ARRAN
2. WALKS ON THE ISLE OF SKYE
3. WALKS IN WESTER ROSS
4. WALKS IN PERTHSHIRE
5. WALKS IN THE WESTERN ISLES
6. WALKS IN ORKNEY
7. WALKS ON SHETLAND
8. WALKS ON ISLAY
9. WALKS ON CANNA, RUM, EIGG & MULL
10. WALKS ON TIREE, COLL, COLONSAY AND A TASTE OF MULL

OTHER TITLES IN PREPARATION

Books in this series can be ordered through booksellers anywhere. In the event of difficulty write to Clan Books, The Cross, DOUNE, FK16 6BE, Scotland.